IMPROVE YOUR SELF-IMAGE

BY UNDERSTANDING

WHAT MAKES SOMEONE ATTRACTIVE

JUSTIN CLOTTEY

Improve Your Self-Image by Understanding What Makes Someone Attractive

Cover by Ravi Verma from rdezines.com

Editing and formatting by Lorraine Reguly from www.WordingWell.com

Dedication

This book is dedicated to all the authority figures, mentors, and examples of excellence in my life. It is because of all of you that I felt inspired enough to invest time and energy in sharing the powerful information in this book.

Table of Contents

JUSTIN CLOTTEY

Preface

Dear reader,

To be successful in life, a good self-image is arguably the most important thing you can have; it will influence how you will live your life.

Whether we wish to admit it or not, the image other people have of us greatly affects how we see ourselves. Why? It dictates how we are treated in the world. It's like feedback. If it's positive, we're on the right track. If it's negative, something about us might be off. Now, to be clear, I'm not referring to the unfounded, illogical disdain others might have for us, such as being hated simply because of the color of your skin, the shape of your hands or other things you have no control over. Rather, I am referring to the image others have of us that is based on how we present ourselves to the world—what we do or say *or* don't do or say. In other words, all the things we have total control over (the subtle as well as the blatant). Bettering ourselves will improve our image in the eyes of others, which will ultimately improve our own self-image.

I'll explain this from another angle. Take a filmmaker, for instance. If their audience doesn't think they are competent at their craft, based on the work they produce, it doesn't matter how good *they* feel they are. The truth is, the individual's value as a filmmaker suffers. This, in turn, will negatively affect their self-image (especially if they've tied their whole identity to filmmaking). However, if their audiences have a *great* impression about them and consequently seek them out, they are deemed to have high value in their domain. That will ultimately reflect in their self-image.

This book is based on the idea of getting people desiring to "seek" you. You see, people seek those that *attract* them. I designed this book to show you what it is exactly that attracts people to others and *why*. However, it's not enough for you to just know a few facts or tips. You should know the ins and outs of what makes a person attractive. This book was made to be a concise, comprehensive guide to help you do just that.

I am someone who has always been fascinated by the concept of attraction. The fact that you're reading this book leads me to believe it is something that interests you as well. More importantly, once harnessed, you will benefit greatly from it.

After you're finished, you will understand why being attractive is important for you to really have success in the world, particularly with other people. Once comprehended, the ease with which you will be able to spark attraction like a light switch (or in some cases, like a dimmer switch) will shock you!

My goal is to get you to the point where *you* become an expert on *why* others find you attractive in *any* given situation—or why they *don't*. From there, you can make the necessary adjustments on the fly, like a football coach in the heat of a match. Think of a mechanic. Imagine one driving their car, when suddenly, it breaks down. How easy would it be for them to diagnose and fix the problem? How little effort would be required to solve the issue? Let's swap out the mechanic for a doctor. Let's say our medical friend fell ill. The idea remains the same. They will make a quick diagnosis and resolution, with minimal external intervention necessary. Why? Because they invested time in learning the ins and outs of their respective fields. I want you to adopt that same ability with attraction—getting to the point where you are able to make quick diagnoses and adjustments to your life!

One of the best ways to learn a complex subject thoroughly is via an organized institution. Consequently, I've set up this book to loosely resemble a mini college or university "program" about human attraction—minus the tests or exams! This is meant to set the stage for you to enter the proper mindset when reading this book. Each chapter is a separate "course" within the "program." In fact, in order to help you get *further* into that head space, I have divided the first eleven chapters into a section called "Bachelor's Degree Program." Those chapters represent all the theory and fundamental knowledge necessary to build upon. The final chapter is put under a section called "Master's Degree Program." During that stage, I want you to start thinking about applying the information you've learned from your "Bachelor's Degree Program." As a bonus, I have included a certificate (degree) at the end of those two sections. I've even left space for you to sign your diploma, once you're done.

At this point, let me warn you about a couple of things. Firstly, what you'll learn about attraction from this book will cause you to see yourself *and* others differently. Secondly, the kind of attraction I discuss herein should not be confused with *the Law of Attraction.* That refers to something different. The focus of this book is solely on person-to-person attraction.

All right, before you officially begin, it is necessary for you to understand how and why I structured the book's comprehensive breakdown of attraction the way I did.

Throughout my career as a teacher, one truth I continuously tell my students is that *everything* in life is connected (whether subtly or overtly). *Everything.* However, in many instances, to understand one specific thing better, you must isolate and examine it individually. The factors of attraction explained in this book work no differently! In other words, to see the full effect of each *individually*, they must be complemented by a few others working in tandem. It's like working out your muscles. You can do exercises that focus on strengthening one specific muscle group. However, that muscle group is never truly working alone. When someone does a bicep curl (an exercise meant to work just the bicep muscles), their back muscles are also engaged (albeit to a lesser extent). The biceps work at their *maximum* capacity when the back (and other muscles) work synergistically with them. It's the same with attraction. Each of the factors are distinct, and can be examined and improved individually. That's why I explain each factor in its own vacuum. However, working together with the others maximizes the overall effect of any one. As you go through the chapters, this will make more sense.

As a final bonus, there is a section at the end of the book called NOTES where you can jot down any ideas or points that stand out to you that you can start applying to your life.

With that said, I wish you the best of luck on your journey.

Yours truly,

Justin Clottey

JUSTIN CLOTTEY

SECTION ONE:

BACHELOR'S DEGREE PROGRAM

JUSTIN CLOTTEY

Chapter 1: What is Attraction?

To start, let's break down *what* attraction is and what it looks like.

Simply put, attraction is the *emotional* pull toward someone. The key word here is *emotional*. Like any emotion, its *duration* and *intensity* will vary. It can last a while or be very short-lived. It can continue over a long period of time or be just an instant spark. It can be felt powerfully, minimally, or anywhere between the two. One can be attracted to a person they've known for many years. A person can also be attracted to someone they've known for ten seconds. One can be attracted to someone they've never seen before. An individual can be sexually attracted to a person. They can be attracted to someone platonically. A person can be attracted to someone related to them. The list goes on.

Throughout this book, I used "attractive," "attracted to," and other like terms. Whenever I've used these, it's strictly a reference to the *emotional pull* someone feels towards someone else (as per the description in the above paragraph).

Conversely, when I've used terms like "repelled by," "repulsed by," or other like terms, it's a reference to the desire for someone to distance themselves from someone else as a consequence of being turned off by them—the polar opposite of being attracted. Like with attraction, the *intensity* of being repulsed will vary.

What Does Attraction Look Like?

There are several indicators of a person being attracted to someone else. Here are just a few of them:

- A fixed gaze on them when they move
- The "tuning out" of everything else when they speak
- Frequently talking about them
- A burning desire to hang out or work with them
- The admiration that overflows like water in a clogged sink at the thought of them

The list goes on.

Some people are adept at sparking attraction with just about anyone they meet. Others can only ignite it with little intensity. Undoubtedly, you have felt one or more of the aforementioned statements toward *someone*. Conversely, whether you know it or not, *you've* caused one or more of those descriptions in other people as well. Remember, the key with attraction is the emotional pull towards someone. There are countless behaviors people will do when they are emotionally drawn by someone. These actions are as diverse as the people doing them. To simplify it for you, all behaviors resulting from attraction can be tied to one or both of the following words: excitement and admiration.

Love vs. Attraction

It is particularly important I stress that *attraction* and *love* are not the same. A lot of people mistakenly use them as interchangeable terms. For instance, it is very common to hear a spouse explain how they divorced their partner because they didn't *love* them anymore. More often than not, a loss of *attraction* is what they are referring to. They are referring to the excitement, the butterflies in their stomach, etc. that was lost. That is attraction, not love.

So, what's the difference? Simply put, love is a choice, while attraction is not. We consciously make the decision to love someone else, through our actions and our words. Furthermore, there is an intent behind love that is rooted in unselfish motives. The English language does an injustice to the many different types of love that exist, because it merely captures all of them in one word. I'll briefly explain a couple. There is the type love typically shown to someone like a friend or a brother ("philia" in Greek), such as spending time together at a bar, allowing them to borrow your car, and so on. There is also the self-sacrificial love where someone would sacrifice their life on behalf of another person ("agape" in Greek). All of these are conscious decisions rooted in unselfishness, regardless of how a person is *feeling*.

Like love, attraction has different types (as you'll learn through this book). In contrast, attraction is the *feeling* that you can't quite describe, which draws you to another person through by what seems like a magnetic pull. When you're attracted to someone, you *feel* the desire to be around them and to engage with them. Where love is the *conscious choice* we make to be around a person, attraction sparks an emotional desire to invest our time and energy into them.

People often get the two confused because they complement each other very well. It is easier for a person to love someone they are emotionally drawn to.

Think of attraction as a lubricant. If you've ever been on a water slide on a hot summer day, you know how hard it is to slide down when there is little to no water present. At times, you almost have to *force* yourself to slide down, dragging and rubbing your bare skin on the slide, just to move. It's still possible to slide down but it requires more effort! What happens if you add water to that surface? It's a different ball game. You slide down like a rocket. Love is the slide. Attraction is the water.

Do you need to be attracted to someone in order to love them? No, you don't. However, it's much easier when the two are present together.

To contrast love and attraction even further, I'll apply *you* to an example. Let's take two very well-known people: Michael Jordan and the late

Mother Teresa. We'll compare them to close family members of yours, your mother and brother, for instance. If you don't have either of these, use two family members you're close with. Now, from simply reading the names "Michael Jordan" and "Mother Theresa," what thoughts come to mind? Really think about this. Take a moment. Even if you only loosely know who they are, the mere sight of their names is sure to bring up emotions (however subtle). Which ones? I'd bet a lot of money they are emotions linked to either excitement or admiration. What you feel, though, is not love; it's attraction. You are drawn to them emotionally, through no conscious effort of your own. Love would involve you having some sort of access to them.

Enter those two close family members. It is likely you love your mother and brother. Why? You *consciously choose* to do things for them, out of unselfish motives. If these motives are actually rooted in selfishness (which only you would truly know), I'd argue that it's not even *real* love. That, however, is a topic for another book. Now, where attraction is concerned, does this mean you *can't* be emotionally drawn to these two family members? Of course, you still can. In fact, to find out, simply determine if they create feelings of excitement and/or admiration in you. To whatever degree they do (or don't) lies your attraction to them.

Can the love and attraction dynamic be unilateral? Unfortunately, as we see far too often in the world, yes. In other words, one person can love and be attracted to another and not have it reciprocated in the slightest.

Can you *only* love someone you know well? No. You can love anyone (a stranger, an authority figure, *even* a Michael Jordan)! As I said before, though, love involves some sort of access to the person.

Succinctly summarized, attraction involves your emotions and love involves intentional, unselfish behavior.

Factors of Attraction

Attraction is like a professional sports club. There are so many different facets that make the club what it is: the training staff, the physiotherapists, the team doctors, the departments for advertising and human resources, the facility's maintenance crew; the list goes on. Although they are relevant, many of these facets are an afterthought (if even a thought at all). However, the actual team players playing the sport are the crown jewels or main attraction of the club (pardon the pun). They are the reason the club exists *and* who the focus is primarily on.

Attraction is no different. With over seven billion people on the Earth (at the time this book was written), there are so many different subtleties to what attracts any one person to another. However, there are eight "main attractions" of attraction. The players, if you will, that are responsible for creating the *strongest* emotional pull in others, no matter which way you slice it. In fact, these eight factors cross cultural, language, gender, racial, and religious barriers. They even transcend class or socioeconomic status. With that said, let's meet our starting lineup:

1. Certainty
2. Ease
3. Balance
4. Brevity
5. Mastery
6. Lightheartedness
7. Reputation
8. Physical appearance

There are few points to understand about this team. Like with any other team, all members play an important and different role for the collective whole. However, within specific contexts or among different people, some factors will shine brighter and be more emphasized than others. With that said, it is important to note that a person deemed "attractive" doesn't necessarily need to "display" all eight factors. In some cases, one or two will spark massive attraction. It's all in the eye of the beholder. If someone is *perceived* to display all eight at an ideal level, though, their attractiveness (ability to draw people to them emotionally) will shoot through the roof.

A society (with its cultural norms and biases) along with the perspective of any one individual, are the biggest influences on the aforementioned.

In fact, individual perspective is a recurring theme you'll notice throughout the book.

The final significant point to understand about attraction is that just because someone displays all or most of the eight factors doesn't automatically mean that that person will automatically be sought after. In other words, if someone is highly attracted to you, that doesn't always mean they will seek you out over someone they are *less* attracted to. To make this point more palatable, I'll use food as an example. I hope you're reading this book on a full stomach!

If someone is hungry, it is *highly likely* they will try to find something to eat, although that is not a guarantee. Some people will *choose* not to eat, despite their hunger. On the other hand, there are those who will eat even when they are *not* hungry! Both of these scenarios apply to attraction. Sometimes, people will seek those they are *not* attracted to. Attraction simply increases the likelihood that they will.

By this point, you should have a good grasp of *what* attraction is. In the next chapter, we will look at why attraction is important to understand. You may not even be aware of some of the reasons!

Key Takeaways

> Attraction is the emotional pull toward someone we experience. It causes us to

feel the desire to be around them, to engage with them, and to invest our time and energy into them.

➤ There is a distinct difference between love and attraction (although they may appear similar).

➤ People are *most* drawn to eight characteristics in other people, which are: certainty, ease, balance, brevity, mastery, lightheartedness, reputation, and physical appearance.

JUSTIN CLOTTEY

Chapter 2: Why is Attraction Important?

Humans are social beings. Therefore, developing relationships is very important. In fact, one can have no money nor resources to their name. However, if they have the *"right"* relationships, they can obtain almost anything they want through the people they know. Take a second to let that sink in. Our relationships are key.

We also live in an age where technology has exposed us to almost every corner of the globe. We can meet people and find out about their lives through a variety of platforms, like never before! Gone are the days when, to meet people, you actually needed to step out of your house. Networking can be done under a warm blanket, on one's bed, with the tap of a screen. With this ease of accessibility to others comes massive opportunities. Take business, for instance. The heart of business is social interactions. The Internet has made both finding and starting a business you're interested in almost seamless. What about the world of dating? Countless platforms have become available to provide exposure to people you might desire romantically. For platonic connections, meet-up groups are published on websites to join people with shared interests, and they are growing with each passing day. The list goes on.

Like with any solution or advancement, new problems arise. More accessibility equals more competition. Whether within the context of establishing business, platonic, or romantic relationships, the competition continues to grow. Subconsciously, although many are unaware, people ask themselves the following question when interacting with others: "Given *all* the available options to whom to give my time and energy, how much, *if any*, should I give *this* person?" The overwhelming majority of the time, the answer comes down to attraction level. That is why it is so important to learn what *attracts* other people.

As I mentioned at the beginning of the chapter, at our core, we are social beings. Therefore, learning how to socialize properly is a *necessity* more so than just a mere good idea.

For instance, picking one's nose when speaking to someone is highly frowned upon in many societies in the world. Let's say Georgia blatantly picks her nose while speaking to Damian. Does the fact that she does this threaten his life? Not at all. What it *does* is *discourages* Damian from further associating with Georgia. Furthermore, it will leave an imprint on Damian. For future encounters with Georgia, he will remember that repulsive behavior and hesitate to associate with her. In other words, Georgia has now repelled Damian from her (the opposite of attract). Regardless of how smart she is or what she can offer him, that one behavior has essentially put a "dent" in the relationship. Whether it was a business, platonic, or romantic relationship, damage has been done. That's how powerful attraction (or lack thereof) is!

Take yourself. When socializing with others, you will try your absolute best to *never* pick your nose in front of them, no matter how strong the urge. Whether you learned this social etiquette from your parents or vicariously through others, it's always at the back of your mind (whether you're aware or not).

The list of repulsive behaviors when socializing is extensive.

At this point, I'll ask you a pivotal question.

As we were taught by society what *not* to do to push people away, wouldn't it be *just as* important to understand that which would actually *draw people to you,* to make them want to socialize with you more?

I'll let you answer that question. As you do, I want to bring to light a couple of the key principles that apply to all types of socialization.

Principles of Socialization

Principle #1: People are *most* receptive to someone if they are drawn to them. I'll write that again because of how important it is. People are *most* receptive to someone if they are *drawn* to them. When that is the case, four things usually happen: (1) a person's words hold more weight, (2) others have more interest in them, (3) others give them more of their time and attention, and (4) often, others will even be more willing to give that person the benefit of the doubt in a suspect situation.

Principle #2: It's not so much about *what* someone does or says but more about *who* is doing and saying it and *how* they are doing and saying it. This is an important principle to understand about person-to-person interactions because of the fact that our words and our actions can frequently become misconstrued. For instance, you can say to someone: "What you just did was really smart!" Depending how you say it and your relationship to them, that one message will convey different meanings.

- **Scenario 1:** You can say it in a sincere, heartfelt way, while you put your hand on their shoulder
- **Scenario 2:** You can say it in a sarcastic, dragged-out manner, while rolling your eyes

- **Scenario 3:** You can say it in a surprised, high-pitched voice, with a shocked expression on your face

These are just a few of the many possible ways to say the *exact same* sentence to someone, but each will have a *totally* different meaning, depending on *how* you say it. If you throw into the equation who is saying it, the meaning can change again—whether it's said by your best friend, an authority figure, or someone you aren't fond of (to name a few).

Depending on someone's attraction level to you, it will determine how receptive they are to how you interact with them. In other words, the more someone is attracted to you and the way you *do* and *say* things, the more receptive they will be to you. In this sense, *what* you say and do holds little importance within the interaction with someone. That part goes over so many people's head causing them to socialize "wrongly." *What you say and do to a person matters far less than who you are, in their eyes, and how you interact!* That's why it is so important to understand what draws people in emotionally!

You can apply these principles wherever possible in your own life. Doing this will increase other people's receptiveness to you. Your potential client is more willing to seek out your business *and* recommend you to friends. The person on the street you ask for directions is more likely to want to give *you* their time. The receptionist who sees thousands of people a day will give *you* special treatment. That person you find very desirable will beg *you* to spend time with them. The friend who doesn't like the genre of movie *you* recommended is more open to check it out. This list goes on. People are *most* receptive to you if they are *drawn* to you. We are social beings and cannot go through life alone. Learning what draws people in to increase their desire to forge and sustain relationships with you is essential to being successful in life.

Learn what Lubricates the Slide

I'll conclude this chapter with the example of the slide from Chapter 1.

Let me take you back to that painful sliding experience on that hot summer day. Remember, love is our big blue slide and attraction is the water. The agony of trying to slide down it occurs with little to no water present. It is possible to descend but only through much forced effort. Would you want to continue going to that slide, given how much of a chore it is to go down it? It's like going to a meeting and listening to a speaker you are not drawn to, like talking to a stranger on a bus who doesn't emotionally pull you, or like doing a business deal with someone you aren't attracted to. You'd probably take the politically correct path and show love toward these individuals, giving them a little of your time and attention, but it would be a painful experience. However, if you put water on that slide (throw attraction into the equation), not only does "sliding" become easier, but you will look forward to doing it more in the future.

I want you to take your socialization with others to a high level. Reading this book, understanding the eight factors of attraction, and increasing your attractiveness are all steps in that direction.

In the next eight chapters, we will unpack the eight factors that lubricate slides all around the world.

Key Takeaways

> It is very important to ask yourself the following question: Just as you were taught by society what *not* to do to push people away, wouldn't it be just as important to understand that which would actually *draw* people to you, to make them want to socialize with you more?

> The amount of time and energy you give to another person extremely depends on your level of attraction to that person.

> Understanding the eight factors of attraction will help you take your

socialization and relationships with others to the next level.

Chapter 3: Certainty

What is Certainty?

I have no doubt that when the word "certainty" comes to mind, you have an idea of what it means. However, when it comes to people, it is a lot more nuanced than you might think.

In simple terms, *certainty is the absence of hesitation in speech and behavior.*

Now, let's unpack this further.

This "lack of hesitation," as I describe it, stems from a belief which a person is certain about. This belief is not something innate; people either get their certainty from seeing evidence or merely fabricating it from thin air.

For example, someone can be at a stoplight behind a big truck that blocks their view of whatever is ahead. Although they can't see the light, if they see the cars around them moving forward, they will *believe* it is green. The driver has evidence. The following week, that *same* driver can be alone, approaching the same traffic light, in a snowy blizzard. Although they can't see the color of the light, they will simply believe it is green and move through the intersection without stopping. In both cases, there was no questioning or hesitation.

There is also no limit to how much certainty a person can have (or display). Certainty is akin to a sliding scale that can go up and down at any point in time. For some, their environment greatly affects their certainty. For others, their certainty stays the same, no matter what. It is *that* unwavering certainty that captivates others. In *that* certainty, there is an absence of hesitation in speech and behavior.

Now, let's continue unpacking the nuances.

What Certainty Looks Like

To make sure you and I are on the same page (no pun intended), it is necessary to understand what exactly this captivating factor of attraction looks like.

At face value, certainty is simply displayed at any given time, and there are six distinct lenses through which a person's certainty can be seen:

1. Body language
2. Approach to specific activities
3. Carrying out specific activities
4. General daily life
5. Passion
6. Response to a challenge

We'll look at each one of these.

1. Body Language

Body language refers to how our subconscious mind communicates to the outside world using our bodies. In and of itself, it truly is fascinating, if you think about it. We speak consciously using our mouths, while our brains speak through our bodies, without us even knowing. In addition, we have the ability to override it at any time (like a parent interrupting and speaking on behalf of their child).

Where certainty is concerned, our bodies display specific types of gestures (or lack thereof) to convey how much of it we feel. As a rule of thumb, the more certain a person feels, the less hesitative or fidgety movements they will do. Rather, you'll see very smooth movements or little movement at all. This makes sense, as it falls in line with the definition given at the beginning: *certainty is the absence of hesitation in speech and behavior.*

Here is a chart that will help you understand the major movements (or lack thereof) of someone displaying certainty and uncertainty.

Body Language Action	Certain	Uncertain
Eye contact	- Will be consistently fixed on that or who the focus is	- Consistent deviation from the that or who the focus is on

Body Language Action	Certain	Uncertain
Hand movement	- Very little to no fidgeting - Hand motions are used to accentuate what they are saying (how much or if at all depends on the individual)	- Constant fidgeting, often with an external source (like an object, hair, or clothing) - Subconscious scratching of parts of their body
Leg movement	- When stationary, like when seated or standing, legs will be typically spread apart - Very little to no movement (i.e., no pacing back and forth) - When walking to a target, pace is steady and direct	- Swaying and pacing back and forth - When walking, pace is inconsistent and/or there is no clear, direct movement to a given target

Body Language Action	Certain	Uncertain
Voice	- Voice tone is steady (whether loud or quiet, high-pitched, or deep)	- Constant stuttering and use of filler words like "uh" or "um"

As you can see, there is a distinct contrast between "certain" and "uncertain" body language. The former has the power to draw people in like a magnet and the *reason* for this will be discussed later in the chapter. Keep in mind, when a person is certain, that doesn't necessarily mean they will display *all* of the above characteristics. The same is true for when a person is uncertain. The chart explains what *generally* will be evident.

2. Approach to Specific Activities

How a person behaves in the lead-up to doing activities is very telling of how certain they are. *Again, the more certain, the less evident the hesitation is, in speech or behavior.* To help you get a clear picture of what this looks like, let's take two people who are going to give a speech (everyone's favorite activity).

Both Farhana and Marie are delivering their respective speeches in front of 1000 people each, on the same day. There is a major difference in how each spends their night prior to the day of the speech. Overall, Farhana displays less hesitative behavior compared to Marie. Why? Marie is uncertain about how her speech will go, while Farhana is certain.

How does this look?

The night before, Marie paces up and down the house, rehearsing her speech. Farhana doesn't. When practicing, Marie stutters and forgets some of her lines. Farhana sits comfortably on her couch, watching television. When her boyfriend comes to see her that night, all Marie talks about with him is how nervous she feels about her speech the next day. When Farhana's boyfriend comes to see her, she doesn't even bring it up. The only time she mentions it is during one of the commercials, when he asks her: "Are you ready for your speech?" To that, all she responds is "Yes," with no further mention of it for the rest of the night. Marie's hands tremble all night, right up until she actually speaks the next day. Farhana's do not.

What makes Farhana certain about her speech, while Marie feels the opposite? It doesn't matter. The most important is *that* she is certain.

Like I mentioned above, certainty comes from belief. Farhana believes in her ability to deliver her speech the next day. That's why she shows little to no hesitative behavior (consciously and subconsciously) the day before the speech.

A *logical* explanation for Farhana's certainty and Marie's lack thereof, would be that the former has done this same speech 85 times prior, in front of the same number of people. The latter, on the other hand, is doing her speech for the first time. After doing the same speech 85 times, Farhana has ironed out all her mistakes and knows exactly what to expect from the audience, which breeds extreme certainty prior to her 86th time.

Keep in mind, this is the logical scenario. There are people who would be just as certain as Farhana during their first time delivering a speech. Yes, these people exist. No, they are not magical beings. It doesn't matter where the belief comes from. When it's present, certainty will follow. When certainty is there, the hesitative behaviors leading up to the activity will decrease. To people watching or involved in the lead-up to activities, the absence of hesitation is extremely attractive.

3. Carrying Out Specific Activities

How does certainty look when carrying out specific activities? You guessed it—with little to no hesitation present. Our friends Farhana and Marie helped us get a visual of the "approach." Now, Jarvis will help us examine certainty, in the midst of doing an activity.

Jarvis plays semi-professional basketball with a local club team, the New Orleans Tornados. Jarvis is certain about his shooting ability. In games, when he gets the ball at the three-point line, he never hesitates to let it fly. Jarvis always shoots the ball, without a second thought, regardless of the space between him and his defender or what the crowd's reactions are.

Irrespective of whether he makes or misses the basket, or whether the defender blocked his shot on the play prior, Jarvis remains certain. Why? Like Farhana, he simply believes in himself and his abilities. Whether his beliefs came from practicing three hours a day, seven days a week, *or* if he fabricated them out of nowhere, the result is the same: his belief is unwavering. How do you think his teammates respond? They willingly keep giving him the ball!

When you are in the presence of someone displaying certainty with what they are doing as a collective, you are more likely to comply and support what they want to do (almost without even giving it a second thought). In this example, it was Jarvis's teammates passing him the ball.

Let's look at an example that involves *you* buying a product. Which product? Allow me to explain.

Let's forget Jarvis for a second and go back to Farhana and Marie. One after the other, both approach you to sell you the same product. For the sake of this example, it is a product that you have been actively seeking. The two had pretty much the same pitch (very similar wording, etc.). Furthermore, both displayed body language of certainty. The difference is that Farhana told you, without a shadow of a doubt, that her product would give you the results you're looking for. She then proceeded to say that she was so sure, that she'd give you 100% of your money back if it didn't. Marie, on the other hand, told you that she was *quite* sure you would get the results you were looking for and that she'd heard good things about it. Unlike Farhana, she did not offer a money-back guarantee.

Farhana's product is $10 more than Marie's. Who would buy from?

I'm 100% sure you would purchase from Farhana *even though* it will cost you more. Why? You are so drawn strongly to her level of certainty that you will even comply with her higher price tag. She is so certain, that she is even willing to reimburse you if you don't get the result you want. You naturally think to yourself, *This must work*. In contrast, despite Marie's lower price and similar sales pitch, based on *her* certainty being less than her counterpart's, you'll choose Farhana's product because she is *more* certain.

4. General Daily Life

Certainty can be seen in how someone behaves when they have no specific obligations—a person's default state, if you will. As with the four other "lenses," the more certain in themselves someone is, the less you see them hesitate. Where a person's belief was previously rooted in their ability to do the specific task, here it is rooted in their potential ability to attain or handle whatever comes on their path. In other words, they *feel* equipped. This is what people would deem a "confident" person. Keep in mind, there's no "one specific look" to this certainty. It can take the form of loud and blatant behavior, quiet and understated behavior, or anything in between. There is a common thread, though. There is a directness, a flow, and an ease to them. I go into detail about ease in Chapter 4. Whether you realize it or not, this draws in other people powerfully. Where does it come from? Simply believing (via evidence or mere decision).

5. Passion

When someone is internally driven to accomplish a specific task in their life, they will exude certainty. The more motivated they are, the more the certainty is within them. This is what we refer to as passion.

Furthermore, the higher the internal pull is to achieve their goal(s) or "mission," the less they allow themselves to get distracted by things (or people) that aren't directly connected. Their life has purpose and meaning.

Passion can be very singular in nature or it can be a collection of smaller passions leading to one larger, underlying devotion. For instance, wanting to be the best basketball player in history is a sole focus, whereas being driven to do charity work, motivational speaking, and teaching children with autism all point to a deeper drive, to actively make the world a better place, and consists of smaller components.

Passion develops in a few ways. It can develop it slowly, over time (such as someone finding out at the age of 40 what they are truly driven to do). It can be inspired by an external source (such as watching someone else do something and desiring to achieve the same thing). It can evolve over time (such as originally wanting to be the best at something, then evolving to wanting to help *others* become the best at the same thing). It can also be obvious from a young age.

Regardless of how passion develops, it creates certainty, which strongly draws others.

6. A Response to a Challenge

The final lens through which certainty can be seen is when a person responds to a challenge.

A person's certainty (or lack thereof) is reflected in how they respond when being challenged. This can be a challenge from another person or when they are in a situation that is not going in their favor. Someone who is very sure of what they believe to be true will not hesitate when being challenged. This can be subtle or exaggerated. They will stick to what they believe and state that without faltering.

Where attraction is concerned, how an attractive a person is perceived in their response to being challenged is a very intriguing one. It can go powerfully either way. This is where *weighted certainty* plays a factor. I'll explain that a little later.

Certainty when being challenged is attractive within three contexts. The first is within a leader or subordinate context. Here, the subordinates (or those depending on the one in leadership role) see the certainty from their leader being challenged as very attractive. It is reassuring to them. The second is within the context of romantic attraction. I'll go into that in detail in Chapter 11. The third context is when there is a gray area—for instance, when there is a debate and there is no clear-cut answer. The more certainty a person can display, the more attractive they are perceived, especially to those who are neutral. This is why, during elections, you often see candidates who stay firm on issues that they are challenged on sway the neutral voters toward them. Often, a candidate's certainty will override the fact that their stance is slightly controversial and win them a vote anyway.

When certainty is shown on the wrong side of a black-and-white issue, it has the opposite effect of attraction. To illustrate, we'll stay on the idea of debates. People are turned off when someone who is clearly in the wrong is being challenged and they continue to stay firm in their "wrong" viewpoint. They are less likely be receptive to what you have to say.

To paint a clearer picture, we'll bring in two more people: Talib and Miguel. Both got into a heated debate with a few people watching. Talib believes the earth is flat. Miguel questions him on that assertion. Miguel believes the Earth is round. Despite the fact Miguel provides ample evidence to support this claim, Talib does not waver from his beliefs. At times, during the interaction, Talib expressed himself calmly. During other points, he raised his voice. Regardless, Talib doesn't hesitate with respect to what he believes nor does he change his mind at all. This behavior is a turn-off because Talib's beliefs are clearly in the wrong.

There you have the five lenses through which people's certainty can be seen.

Through the last lens (response to a challenge), I was able to steer you to the idea of debates and the perception of the debaters. I used it to show how a person's certainty can be viewed as not attractive (contrary to how it is viewed through the other lenses). I explained that, where attractiveness is concerned, a person whose certainty is rooted in the wrong side of a black-and-white issue will be seen as unattractive. They would repel people and even turn them off. That is logical enough. Now, I'll show how that isn't always the case. In some cases, if a person's certainty is strong enough, they can emotionally draw *many* people to them who would have otherwise been repelled. This will happen *even if* they are clearly in the wrong. Let me show you what I mean.

An Exception to the Rule

It is highly probable you have heard of Adolf Hitler. You likely have an idea of how much power he had for large stretch of his life. However, he wasn't always *that* powerful. The question then is: How did he get there? I'm aware there were different factors that contributed, but if you boil it down to its core, it came down to his certainty.

You see, Adolf was part of the German military during World War One. At the time, he wasn't thought to be anything special. He didn't come from a wealthy background. He wasn't tall (by many people's standards) or exceptionally handsome, nor was he exceptionally intelligent. He even dressed like the average man for his time. Yet, he became one of the most powerful and influential men in modern history.

How is it that so many became captivated by him? Why were so many people drawn to him? Again, it was his certainty. He was known for speaking with conviction and passion about his radical views. Yes, there were many within the economically decimated Germany that had shared his views. However, most of the German population were against his radical, Anti-Semitic ideas. Yet he, slowly but surely, drew people to him. People were captivated by the certainty in his message. It was through that that he was able to fuel the Anti-Semitic propaganda which was ultimately responsible for the atrocities many millions of Jews faced. If that wasn't enough, the Nazi party which Hitler led pushed the ideology that the Aryan race was the most superior of all—those with white skin, blond hair, and blue eyes.

Although Adolf had only one of those three physical characteristics, people were drawn to him so much, he was made the face of this "superior" race!

Of all the possible illustrations I could have chosen, this is the perfect one to show just how powerfully certainty can draw people in emotionally. Although he was clearly in the wrong, Adolf's certainty is what drew people to him the most. He isn't an anomaly. There have been countless leaders throughout history that have drawn millions (whether for good or for evil) to them, through their unwavering views and behaviors.

More Nuances of Certainty

There are two other nuances that I need to explain before I get into *why* certainty is so attractive:

1) Arrogance
2) Weighted certainty (which includes authenticity/inauthenticity)

Let's continue unpacking.

1) Arrogance

Although both can appear similar, there is a distinct difference between arrogance and certainty.

Arrogance is certainty to the extreme. It disregards everything else. Those who are arrogant are very narrow-focused. Remember how I stated a few lines earlier that the two can look similar? Most of the time it comes down to perception.

Let's go back to Farhana and her night leading up to her speech. To some, Farhana would be perceived as certain while to others, she'd be perceived as arrogant. It's all in the eye of the beholder. The bottom line is that arrogance is unattractive and certainty is attractive.

2) Weighted Certainty

I briefly mentioned weighted certainty earlier. What exactly is it? Simply put, it is a term I use to describe a person's certainty with some form of credibility to back it up.

To make this clear, we'll go back to Farhana. As I stated earlier, a logical reason for her certainty leading up to her speech was a consequence of having done it in front of 1000 people 85 times prior. For the sake of this explanation, we're going to say that was, in fact, the case. With that as the backdrop, I'll explain (through a logical example) how weighted certainty would be perceived.

Let's examine this from the perspective of the representatives of the company who hosted the event she spoke at. During the interview process, they would have been drawn to Farhana because of the weighted certainty she displayed during their vetting process. Make no mistake about it, if she presented them her resume, revealing she had done this 85 times prior but *didn't* convey certainty, she wouldn't have gotten the opportunity. It's the *certainty* that drew the representatives to her. Her resume just adds weight (credibility).

Now, let's put Marie in the same situation. If Marie had conveyed the same level of certainty during her interview process, she would have lost out to Farhana. Why? Marie had no prior experience. Farhana had a ton.

Unweighted certainty will still draw people in, but it will usually lose to the same level of weighted certainty.

Authenticity vs. Inauthenticity

Authenticity is very interesting. It is a by-product of certainty. Essentially, authenticity is when a person is being their true self. They don't hold back who they are and are always honest. This is attractive. In fact, it can almost be considered a separate factor for attraction. However, it falls under the scope of weighted certainty.

A person who is authentic will be certain, by default. In and of itself, authenticity doesn't have the power to pull people in emotionally. That is, if we just look at it as a vacuum, not considering what exactly one is being honest about. However, the certainty *tied* to authenticity is what draws people in—the "I know who I am, take it or leave it" mindset. Using the example of "I am a bank robber. I have been and always will be," the average person isn't draw to someone who steals money from banks. Yet, people will be attracted to their attitude of not caring what others think. They are so sure of themselves that they don't need to lie about who they are or how they think. *That* adds weight to their certainty in people's eyes because it's coming from a genuine place. People are drawn emotionally to that.

Moving to the other side to inauthenticity, we can get a clearer picture of how it shows a lack of certainty (specifically weighted certainty) and thereby repels people.

People don't like being lied to or deceived by others. The reason folks are inauthentic is because of a lack of certainty in themselves and their ability to handle an outcome. People will make the association that if they are lying about one thing, they could be lying about something else. This makes the brain classify inauthentic people as uncertain people. In turn, they are repelled by such people. It's like walking on a plank bridge and one of the planks towards the beginning falls off. You will instantly be turned off to the idea of continuing to walk on that bridge because it has already shown you one part of it cannot be trusted.

Why is Certainty Attractive?

Now that we've explored what certainty is and what it looks like with all its nuances, let's look at *why* it's so attractive. We're almost at the bottom of the certainty bag.

Let's keep unpacking.

Something you must understand about our brains is that it lives on associations. In other words, it constantly links one thing to another (whether logical or not). It does this subconsciously.

Those who are naturally highly emotional aren't adept at separating their conscious brain with logic and simply rely on the associations their brains make to direct their behavior. That is why they will act in ways that sometimes later make no sense. The associations trigger emotions which pull them to one thing or the other.

On the other hand, those who are better able to detach from the associations their brains make are less "emotional." Consequently, more often than not, they make decisions independent of them. The separation can be extremely difficult because our brains are hardwired to make associations. In theory, these associations are to make survival easier. *In essence, it is these associations that make the eight factors talked about in this book so powerful.*

Certainty is so attractive to us humans because our brains link it to strength and reliability.

Before you drive a car, you want to be sure that it won't break down on you while you're driving. You want to know it's strong enough to support your weight when you sit in it. You want to know that when you turn the steering wheel to the left, that the wheels will turn left *every time.*

How would you feel if the car wasn't strong or reliable? You'd be worried. You'd hesitate to even use it. In fact, you'd completely steer clear of it (no pun intended). Whether you know it or not, certainty is the number one thing you look for in a car.

Our brains make that same association to people. We highly value strength and reliability in our lives. It makes sense then, at a subconscious level, that we are drawn strongly to those people who represent these qualities. This is why, for instance, "mob mentality" exists. A multitude of individuals will subscribe to any ideal or belief because *many* others are certain about it. A uniform group belief (whether correct or otherwise) gives a sense of reliability. Whether through means that are negative, positive, right, or wrong, reliability and strength give us that comfort and peace of mind all the same. The brain doesn't care how you get it. As long as it's strong and reliable, the brain will urge you to move toward it.

People light up when they are in the presence of a person who is demonstrating certainty. They will deem that person as "reliable" and "strong." As a result, they are naturally drawn to them. That is why certainty is so powerful and attractive.

Key Takeaways

> Certainty is the lack of hesitation in speech and behavior.

> ➤ Certainty in people can be seen through their body language, their passion, their approach to and when carrying out specific activities, their general daily life, and their response to a challenge.

> ➤ Our brains love strength and reliability. You are drawn to people who display certainty because your mind associates it to those two qualities. That is why certainty is so powerful and attractive.

JUSTIN CLOTTEY

Chapter 4: Ease

What is Ease?

Simply put, ease is the display of smoothness, poise, and elegance with which someone carries themselves. Whether for mere moments or as a consistent state, its emotional pull is nothing short of alluring. People who display ease demonstrate the "less is more" principle. A lesser amount of effort for a favorable result is *always* more attractive than *lots* of effort for the same result.

What Does Ease Look Like?

Here are a couple of illustrations to give you a sense of what ease looks like:

1) A woman is comfortably sitting down, reading while drinking a coffee. She turns the page of her book in a smooth, poised manner while calmly taking a sip of her beverage. Someone observing this from afar would feel the elegant energy that it gives off.

2) A man's girlfriend complains to him about a negative experience she had that day. She articulates her words very fast, with lots of anger and anxiety in her voice. In one smooth motion, without saying a word, he embraces her. The man then kisses her on the forehead and slowly rubs

her back, all while keeping her in his embrace. His actions calm her down, causing her to mentally put aside her issue and be drawn in emotionally to him.

Ease is one of the eight factors of attraction where its description on a page doesn't do it full justice. Nonetheless, the two above scenarios are meant to give you a picture of the ease I'm talking about—a relaxed behavior and steady demeanor, which together give off a vibe of calmness and control. When you see it, you feel it *instantly*. Interestingly enough, it is easier to identify when someone *doesn't* display ease. Think of someone you know who has ever displayed frantic energy. They don't even have to say a word for you to feel it exude from them.

Like with the other factors of attraction, the nuances of ease can be broken down and examined. We shall do just that. Ease can be best seen through:

1. Body language
2. Interactions
3. General daily life
4. Understated response to adversity

1. Body Language

As I explained in the previous chapter on certainty, your brain will communicate through your body. Here is a chart that breaks down the body language of someone who displays ease (or lack thereof).

Body Language Action	Ease	Unease
Eye contact	- Fixed on the person or point of focus - Controlled, smooth blinking - Eyes are not fully open all the way (not wide-eyed)	- Fast eye twitching - Eyes are wide open
Hand movement	- Motions will be steady and smooth - Very little to no fidgeting, even when using hand motions to accentuate what they are saying (at times, no hand motions will be used at all)	- Constant fidgeting (often with external items, such as hair or clothing) - Subconsciously scratching parts of their body

Body Language Action	Ease	Unease
Head movement	- When focusing on someone, head is fixed straight at target - When head is moving, it is always slow and controlled	- Head swivels constantly, looking in different directions
Tone of voice	- Voice tone is steady (whether loud or quiet) - Pregnant pauses within speech - Not many tonality variations	- Stuttering - Using fillers like "uh" or "um" - Frequent tone fluctuations
Facial expressions	- Smile is not exaggerated and can be more of a smirk	- Different emotions are evident when a new stimulus is introduced

	- Relaxed facial expressions (sometimes even giving an impression of disinterest)	

From the chart, you can see there are some similarities with the body language of certainty, as I discussed in the previous chapter. The major difference is that a person with ease demonstrates a sense of calm and control with everything. With certainty, this is not necessarily the case.

2. Interactions

A person's ease spills into their interactions—not only with other people but interactions with their external environment as well.

I'll start with person-to-person communication.

Someone who has this ease is in no rush to get their words out or influence a conversation. Often, they will allow the other party to do most of the talking. Many times, people who are shy will do this naturally. As a result, they can *unintentionally* give off the same sense of poise and control that a person with ease does. The second most salient aspect is their reactions. When an individual with this type of ease reacts within an interaction, it is always understated. For instance, if something is funny, they may laugh, but not too much. Instead, they may simply smile or smirk.

Their reactions to social tension are also understated. When an issue arises, it's almost as if they are completely unaffected by it. For instance, if someone with ease starts holding the shoulder of a person with whom they are communicating (as a gesture of endearment), they will hold their hand there just a few seconds longer than "normal." To the other person, it may feel awkward. The person displaying ease will, however, remain steady and unbothered by the other person's reaction.

When ease is displayed at just the right level during interactions, it is extremely magnetic in *every* context. When displayed to the extreme, though, it gives the impression of arrogance or aloofness, which is unattractive.

So, how can we tell the difference between "the right amount" and "too extreme"? Well, just like with differentiating certainty from arrogance, it comes down to perception.

Earlier, I gave you a general example of how someone with ease interacts. Now, I will give you two specific ones of well-known people. Both almost always seem to display this magnetic ease that I'm breaking down in this chapter, in *whatever* they do. One is a fictional character and the other is a real person. They are Agent James Bond (007) and the former president of the United States, Barack Obama.

Let's start with James. He always finds himself in dangerous predicaments. Regardless of whether he's on rough terrain or trapped in a room, he is always calm. In certain scenes of his movies, James is tied up to something like a chair in an unknown place. Although he is by himself in a stressful situation, he doesn't panic. Rather, he remains unbothered—no murmuring, no yelling, and no fidgeting. He calmly evaluates the situation he's in. Then, he thinks of possible ways to get out of it and the possible obstacles to avoid. After calmly doing the calculation in his head, he then takes decisive action.

In other scenes, Bond is tasked with taking someone on in physical combat. Again, in those situations, 007 remains poised. Although the adversary makes threats on his life, he doesn't lose his cool or even reciprocate the same belligerent energy. Instead, he calmly responds, expending as minimal effort as possible. He will engage in combat *when* he has to, but in the lead-up, he is always poised and calm.

James is also famous for the scenes where he seduces beautiful, desirable women. In such instances, his ease is on full display. Usually, it's a woman working against him during his main mission and who's playing hard to get throughout their interactions. Whatever the case, he always remains calm and poised. He simply "rides the wave," so to speak. Eventually, the women are taken in by his coolness. Then, well, you can use your imagination to surmise what happens next!

Although James Bond is a fictional character, the cause and effect of ease on others still rings true!

On to Barack. There's probably not a better example of someone who has as much status as he does or who displayed as much poise as he did in the various situations he was in as leader of the free world. I will give you a specific example. In 2009, during an interview, he was in the middle of answering a question as a fly was pestering him. Although he *was* bothered and lost his trail of thought, he remained poised. He calmly waved it away. At one point, he noticed that it had landed on his hand. While staying seated, he killed the fly with one swift swat. He accomplished that without really moving too much. Immediately afterward, the former president was ready to resume the interview and asked the interviewer: "Where were we?" He wouldn't have even called attention to it if those behind the camera had not expressed how impressed they were. There is a video clip of this situation all over the Internet. I suggest you look it up to get a visual of just how calmly he handled the situation. It perfectly displays the "ease" which this chapter talks about, which is highly attractive.

That instance with the fly aside, when giving speeches or interacting with other world leaders, Obama has a coolness to him. He's never visibly fazed. Even when excited, the former leader of the free world never really exaggerated his feelings. When criticized or challenged, he keeps his cool and calmly articulates his way out of the issue. When on camera, there's never an extra expenditure of energy—*ever*.

I could use Barak Obama as an example for almost all the factors of attraction. However, it is his ease that is the most alluring and salient. I would venture to say, during his political campaign, it was the premier quality that caused so many of his supporters to be drawn to him. The ease he displayed (on top of the competency to hold a position in office) is what gave him his edge over other candidates. To see a stark contrast in someone who held the same position, you need look no further than Donald Trump. Regardless of your personal opinion about the forty-fifth president of the United States, one thing cannot be denied about him: his lack of ease in his social interactions. This is especially the case when he is being criticized.

3. General Life

When someone displays ease in their general life, it simply means they go about their life in a poised manner. They never behave in the extremes. Whether happy, sad, excited or anxious, they remain in the same pocket.

4. Understated Response to Adversity

Ease is most attractive when evident in stressful situations. In fact, the more ease displayed in an intense situation, the more attractive it is. I touched on this idea a little earlier. Why? Poise shown in an intense situation shows a starker contrast. Take a painting, for example, of a white silhouette on a beige background. You will still see the difference. However, if you put the same white silhouette on a black background, it is much more pronounced. Ease follows the same principle.

Keep in mind, it's in handling the situation in a calm, smooth manner that's key. Allowing oneself to succumb to the pressure doesn't have the same effect. That is why many professionals know instinctively to keep their calm when dealing with a difficult client or situation. They understand, without being told, that ease and poise go a long way in winning the client over. Why? It is an attractive quality. Conversely, people are repelled by others who can't keep their calm, even in stressful situations.

Distinction between Ease and Certainty

Ease and certainty go together like peanut butter and jelly. However, they are independent of each other.

Let's go back to Farhana and Marie. We know they both delivered a speech in the previous chapter.

Now, let's say they both gave the same speech, using the same exact words, speaking for the same length of time. If you remember, Farhana was extremely certain and Marie was not. As a result, Farhana is better suited to deliver her speech with much more smoothness, poise, and elegance than Marie. Based on how her preparation the night before went, it is more likely that Marie stutters her words, trembles, and unintentionally inserts nervous laughter into her speech. In that scenario, the audience will be more emotionally drawn to Farhana than Marie (although they are delivering the same content). From this example, you can see the clear correlation between ease and certainty.

When someone has the magnetic ease that I've discussed in this chapter, you can be sure they have a high level of certainty as well. It's not necessarily the same the other way around. A high amount of certainty doesn't equate to poise, elegance, and smoothness.

Distinction between Laziness and Ease

Remember the "less is more" principle, which I briefly alluded to earlier in the chapter? It is truly powerful. However, be careful. There is a clear line between being lazy or aloof and displaying ease. Laziness occurs when there is too little concern from a person placed in a situation. This is actually very unattractive because it shows incompetence. How can we tell where the line is? It all comes down to *perception*.

Why is Ease Attractive?

So, why is ease so attractive? As I mentioned in the previous chapter, our brains constantly make associations subconsciously. Our brains highly value reliability and strength. Just like with certainty, our brains associate a calm demeanor and poised behavior with those two things. However, it goes a step further.

Ease is non-threatening. The brain's primary objective is to keep us alive. Therefore, it is subconsciously on high alert for things that it perceives as potentially harmful so we can avoid them. Consequently, it will encourage you to move away from things that are threatening. That's why if you are near an angry lion, your brain will discourage you from approaching it. Even if the lion is calm, your brain is still weary of approaching it because of its *potential* to be dangerous. Your brain will also make this loose association with people. Although we are not always totally repelled by a nervous and frantic demeanor, the opposite qualities will draw us in (especially if it a person who has value to them possesses them).

It is for those two reasons, dear reader, that the more ease someone displays, the stronger the emotion pull they will have on others.

Key Takeaways

- ➢ Ease is the display of smoothness, poise, and elegance with which someone carries themselves.
- ➢ A person's ease can be seen through their interactions, how a person lives their life in a general sense, their body

language, and their understated response to adversity.

➢ Our brains love reliability and that which is non-threatening. Because they associate a person with ease as having these two qualities, we are highly drawn to that person.

JUSTIN CLOTTEY

Chapter 5: Balance

Allow me to introduce to you the most multi-faceted factor of attraction: balance. The underlying rule here is that people are strongly drawn to those who they *perceive* can potentially help them *achieve* or *maintain* balance in their life. You see, everyone looks for balance (consciously or subconsciously) in all areas of their lives.

There are three types of balances, some of which you might not be aware existed. That's okay; your subconscious mind doesn't tell you *everything*. Luckily, you are about to learn what these balances are.

The key is that people are drawn *strongest* to people that represent the type of balance *they* seek at a given time. As you go through this chapter, you'll understand this more.

The three types of balances are:
1. Equalizing balance
2. Counterbalance
3. Visual balance

1. Equalizing Balance

"Equalizing balance" is a term I use to describe how we seek to maintain balance in our lives in terms of *us* relative to *others*. To explain this, let's use the following illustration. Think of your life as a scale that has two sides. One represents what you bring to the table (your values, your beliefs, your energy, etc.). The other side is what others bring to the table. In order for your side to stay at a consistent (comfortable) level, you need people in your life who will help you "maintain the equilibrium" with *the same* or *similar* amount of the aforementioned things. Just like with a real scale, as soon as one of the sides becomes heavier or lighter, you lose the equilibrium and the scale goes out of whack.

That is why people are strongly attracted to those they perceive as sharing similarities to them. Specifically, these include similar mindsets, similar interests, similar outlooks on life, and similar cultural upbringings, although the list goes on. Two strangers who can start up a two-hour conversation about golf will swear they felt an instant "connection" with one another just from that 120-minute long conversation. Although they may never see one another again, they will feel strongly drawn to each to each other. Conversely, they may feel no such way about a co-worker they've known for 10 years.

Furthermore, finding someone for equalizing balance is almost like discovering an extension of oneself. There is a familiarity, which brings comfort. That's why in many instances, a person will gravitate almost exclusively toward people of a similar socio-economic class, culture, or race.

Consequently, it is also why they will shy away from those of differing ones. They are repelled by the inherent unknown or unfamiliarity which they bring. This repulsion comes up in subtle ways.

Let's take the hiring practices of many companies. In a place where the Anglo-Saxon culture has the predominant influence, a name like Kwesi Ebo would discourage the company recruitment team from even considering the resume. They would be more inclined to look at a resume with similar qualifications of a candidate with a name like John Smith. Why? It is a more of a common name within the Anglo-Saxon culture. Hiring someone like that would help maintain equalizing balance within the company (in theory).

The list of subtleties in behavior and attitudes toward those who are perceived to strike that equalizing balance (or not) are endless.

2. Counterbalance

It's highly likely you've heard the statement "opposites attract," at one point or another. In other words, people of opposing personalities often form strong relationships (usually in a romantic context).

Contrary to equalizing balance, this type of balance has to do with attraction to people who characteristics are opposite to yours. As a result, they bring an element to your life that is lacking, to make it more "complete" or *balanced.* Magnets are the best illustration to represent this.

Let's go back briefly to elementary school science class.

Magnets have a "north" and a "south" end. When you put two magnets together, the "north" end of the first magnet is strongly attracted to the "south" end of the second. Why? The movement of the electrons in the north end *complement* the movement of the electrons in the south end. In contrast, the north sides of two magnets will repel each other because they are moving in opposite directions.

The interaction between electrons is the exact same in human interactions. For instance, when two hard-headed people have their own ideas of how a plan should be carried out, they will not get along. In essence, they are moving in opposite directions. If, however, you have one strong-headed person and one who is open-minded in terms of how the plan should be carried out, they will get along much better (moving in the same direction).

Like I touched on earlier, the counterbalance attraction can be best seen in romantic relationships, most notably in the dynamic of masculine and feminine energy (more on this in Chapter 10). That is why some people will exclusively date outside of their race/culture. They *perceive* the potential partners of the other race(s) will bring an aspect their lives that they lack. Within a friendship context, we see counterbalance as well. Often, one friend is more outspoken, while the other is more reserved.

3. Visual Balance

The previous two balance types were obvious and straightforward. This one however, is a little more subtle—and intriguing.

There are two specific areas where visual balance is seen: in people and in clothing. Let's look at each in detail.

People

People are attracted to those who display visual balance. In other words, people who physically display symmetry are highly appealing.

The faces that are most attractive are those where the facial features possess a certain symmetry, such as the distance of the eyes from each other, along with their distance from the nose, etc. Makeup is an excellent tool to manipulate this. It is why many women use it to achieve or enhance the symmetry of their facial features. Similarly, it's the reason for why many men shape and trim their beards and hair. It enhances the symmetry of their whole face, which makes them more visual appealing.

The reason a body that is fit is so visually attractive is because it displays symmetry. This symmetry can be attributed to why fit people are often referred to as "in shape." It is also why models who are chosen to be the face of a clothing line or hair products are always have fit bodies and symmetric facial features. People are strongly drawn to the visual balance and by extension, will be more drawn to the product. Those products sell better with them than without them. In contrast, the body of a person carrying excess body fat looks visually asymmetric, hence why they are not as visually appealing on a subconscious level.

Clothing

This visual balance extends to clothing as well. This why well-fitting, well-ironed clothes look so appealing. Wearing clothing like suits in highly formal events give the body a sense of symmetry.

The nuances with clothing can run very deep (like wearing colors that will complement your skin tone, etc.). I won't get into too much detail about them. The bottom line here is that balance—in all its forms—is the most attractive.

One important thing I will mention is that where clothing is concerned, wearing appropriate clothing at appropriate times plays a huge factor. Wearing the right clothes at the right time can significantly add or subtract attraction where the "balanced" equation is concerned. For instance, at a wedding, one guest shows up in well-fitting khakis and a T-shirt that brings out his skin and well-defined muscular physique. The dress code calls for formal suits for the men and formal dresses for the women, people wouldn't be drawn to him as they would have in a different circumstance. Actually, quite the opposite. The way he is dressed doesn't match the occasion. In other words, it throws off the "balance."

You might be thinking that haircuts and certain clothing that aren't symmetric yet are very attractive. They are attractive for a different reason, outside of visual balance. Billie Eilish is a well-known young musical artist from the United States. Apart from her music, she is known for her style. To say she dresses eccentrically would be an understatement. There is very little symmetry to how she dresses. Yet many people are drawn to her *because* of her wardrobe.

Why?

The reason is not because of the visual balance but a consequence of the other factors discussed in the book. For instance, that type of fashion represents certainty.

As I discussed in the chapter on certainty, people are drawn to the lack of hesitation. The fact that she just dresses how she wants with no regard of opinions displays certainty and could also be an example of equalizing balance (discussed earlier in this chapter). She draws people in who have a similar mindset and lifestyle to hers. Consequently, if you are repelled by how she dresses, this would be a perfect example of that which throws off the balance you want in your life.

Why is Balance Attractive?

Why are we so drawn to "balance"? Our brains love equilibrium—the overall balance of all systems.

The human body has been designed to regulate and maintain equilibrium (through hormones and various bodily functions).

When your body is feeling too hot, you sweat. When your body is too cold, you shiver. When your body needs more food, you will feel hungry. When it has enough food, your brain will signal you are satiated. The list goes on. These are all things your brain does to achieve equilibrium internally.

Your brain looks to achieve the very same externally as well. That is why you are highly drawn to people who your brain perceives will give you that equilibrium in your external life.

Your brain highly values (and seeks out) those who it perceives can best help you achieve equalizing balance and counterbalance.

In terms of visual balance, like I mentioned in previous chapters, our brains are huge on making associations (whether logical or not).

Consequently, those who portray visual balance are highly attractive because your brain associates them as being able to bring "balance" to your life by virtue of the fact that they appear balanced.

Key Takeaways

> ➤ People are strongly drawn to those who they perceive can potentially help them achieve or maintain balance in their life.

> ➤ People look consciously and subconsciously for balance through equalizing balance, counterbalance, and visual balance.

> ➤ Our brains love maintaining equilibrium externally as much as internally. It will urge you to move toward those it perceives as being able to help you achieve and maintain it.

Chapter 6: Brevity

People need to eat. This is an unavoidable fact of life. If you don't eat, you die. Fortunately, many of us *enjoy* eating.

I want you to use your imagination. Take a moment and picture your favorite food. As you think about it, imagine it in your mouth, its flavors hitting your taste buds as it moves along your tongue. Maybe you don't have just one favorite but have several. Picture yourself eating those, too. Vividly imagine all those flavors.

Now, imagine yourself eating that same food but without its flavor. In fact, with no flavor at all. Do you still enjoy it? Everything else is the same—same ingredients, same nutrients, some quantity, same color, same everything—but no taste. You might still eat it, but it won't give you the same excitement you felt in the preceding paragraph. Would you even eat it? Or would you instead search for other foods that gave you that same joy that your now tasteless favorite(s) fail(s) to deliver?

Where am I going with this?

You probably have an idea, given the chapter title and the nature of the above scenario. Let me not keep you in suspense any longer. You see, *brevity* is to attraction as the flavors are to your favorite foods. It is the spice of life, if you will. Without brevity, mystery, rarity, or scarcity, people become dull and predictable. On a grander scale, life becomes bland.

A person can be valuable (essential, even) to your life. However, if there is no brevity, they are like your tasteless favorite food; much appreciated but not appealing. Add the right amount of scarcity to them, and they become unbelievably attractive. Keep in mind, with your favorite food, the flavoring must be just right—not too much but not too little. It is the same with a person and their brevity: not too much scarcity; just the right amount.

The other important parallel between the two is the value to you. If you hate pineapples, it doesn't matter how fresh or how enhanced the taste is, you won't eat them. It's the same with people and brevity; there has to be an already perceived value to you or else their level of mysteriousness will mean nothing.

The goal of the comparison between brevity and your favorite foods was to give you a clearer picture of how it works. With that out of the way, let's unpack what brevity actually is.

What is Brevity?

What exactly is brevity, where people are concerned? Simply put, brevity is when a person reveals themselves in small amounts. Brevity is powerful because it gives people the chance (and incentive) to seek more. The word "brevity" can be replaced with "mystery," "scarcity," or "rarity." They all refer to the same idea.

Think about any trailer to a film that you were eager to see. The goal behind it was to add brevity to the film; to give you a small taste.

People who see a trailer invest their thoughts and their energy into theories as to what will happen in the movie. They never know for sure, so that keeps them thinking and revisiting their theories, thus investing more energy. This puts them into a *cycle of excitement*.

However, if someone told them the ending of the movie, the excitement cycle vanishes. The anticipation is gone, so there is no need to invest further thoughts into it because they know what is going to happen.

Think about the seismic shift in your attraction to the movie. It's the same movie but the "spice" is gone. You may not even want to watch it anymore (like you may not have eaten your favorite flavorless food).

This is how powerful brevity is.

Furthermore, it is this cycle of excitement that is the key when it comes to brevity.

Those who display brevity have the same effect on people. They keep people in a cycle of excitement, even at the mere thought of them. This draws people in powerfully.

What Does Brevity Look Like?

There are three main ways people display brevity:

1. Absence (in a direct sense and in an indirect sense)
2. Withholding information
3. Silence

1. Absence

You have likely heard the saying "absence makes the heart grow fonder," at one point or another. If not, you have now. It essentially means that when you don't have something around, it give you a chance to wonder about and miss it.

The opposite is also true: too much of someone will make you start to hate them.

Think about it. Take anyone you know in your life. Now, imagine they were with you, every second of every day. They are right at your hip. They are there when you shower, when you're on the toilet, when in your car—they are *everywhere*. I'll bet this wouldn't be ideal for you. You'd want your space to breathe.

Therefore, I can make the argument that absence is not only attractive but *necessary*.

When someone is not present for a certain amount of time, others are strongly drawn emotionally to them. The important piece, as I mentioned earlier, is there must a perceived value to that person—or their absence has no affect.

Absence can be broken down into two forms: absence in a direct sense and absence in an indirect sense. Let's look at each in detail.

Absence in a Direct Sense

There are two good friends who haven't seen each other in a year. When they reconnect, they are much more attracted to each other.

Now, take those same two friends. Everything they had achieved absent of each other in the previous scenario, they've still achieved, but within each other's presence. At the one-year mark, they are still friends, but the attraction isn't as strong. For those in a romantic relationship, it's the same idea. The attraction to one another grows much stronger when partners reconvene after an absence from each other. The key here, like I mentioned earlier, is just the right amount of absence. If there is too much, the partner/friend is forgotten.

How do you know what is too long and what is too short an absence? Like with all the other factors, it comes down an individual's perception.

Absence in an Indirect Sense

This refers to an absence in the way a person's scarcity is felt in a specific place. In this situation, it is your absence that makes you attractive to people of that place.

Let me explain this with an example.

Typically, when someone from a developed nation goes to an impoverished country, they are perceived to have money (which equates to value). Consequently, many people there are drawn to that traveler because of the *rarity* they represent (which, in this case, is a person with money). They will receive the treatment that people who are seen attractive get (see Chapter 1). Now, the question is: Is it their actual money that makes the traveler attractive? The instinct is to say yes. After all, money buys happiness, right (wrong!)? Let me explain why it is the mere scarcity of this traveler and *not* the money that draws people to them.

Our traveler in this example, Jarvis (from Chapter 3), was the first foreigner to come from a developed country in 50 years. When he left, his country was in an unfortunate financial situation. A drastic change then occurred within the next 10 years.

For the following decade, the country had its infrastructure turn around, causing it to elevate from its impoverished status. Additionally, within that ten years, there was a huge influx of people from Jarvis's country (the United States). All had a similar or better socio-economic status than Jarvis's. After that decade, Jarvis decided to go back and visit the country. Despite having the same amount of money, clothing, status, etc., his perceived attractiveness went down. Why? His scarcity as a "First-World traveler" isn't felt as much as before.

Now, let's say Jarvis goes to London, England. People are not drawn to him as they were in his first destination, although he has the same amount of money and status as he did there. His scarcity as a "First-World traveler" isn't felt in London.

Therefore, it is a fallacy that people are strongly drawn to money, status, or fame; the draw is to *scarcity*. Take any celebrity, the most famous one you know. People (including you) aren't drawn to that person because of their fame. What is attracting them (and you) is really the scarcity of that type of person in the life of "non-famous" people.

People who have the same level of fame aren't attracted to your chosen celebrity because of fame (because they don't have a scarcity of that type of person in their social circles). Granted, this celebrity can be attractive to others because of one of the *other* seven factors of attraction but it's *not* the fame, status, or money!

2. Withholding Information

Brevity is displayed when people don't reveal all the information about themselves. I mentioned the "cycle of excitement" earlier in the chapter. That is what keeps people drawn to others more than they would have otherwise been. They are constantly wondering and drawing conclusions that *could* be true, but they don't know for sure. This is especially the case when others try to find out information about someone.

For instance, Talib (from Chapter 3), works at an engineering firm. He typically keeps to himself.

One day, he decides to go on one of the many outings he often gets invited to. Usually, he chooses to decline the invitations. On this particular day, he was in a good mood, so he accepted.

His co-workers know nothing about him. He's the only one who has never been on one of the outings. Talib always brings in the biggest clients but is hardly in the office. When he is, he only ever talks about work. This makes others curious about him.

Naturally, they ask him personal questions. He keeps his responses short, never elaborating. In one of his responses, he mentioned how he wrestled a tiger the other week. Again, he offers no elaboration. When one of the co-workers asked him to elaborate on the situation, he got up and expressed his apologies about having to leave. Then he departed, leaving his co-workers feeling additional curiosity.

Whether truthful or not, shy or not, Talib left everyone in the excitement loop because of his brevity. This is powerful. Although they are undoubtedly annoyed with him, his co-workers are even more drawn to him now. He *still* didn't reveal everything about himself, even though he had the opportunity. Don't forget, he had the important prerequisite of perceived value to the group. The interesting thing with situations typical to this, even if Talib had not had that perceived value, just the mysterious aura surrounding him would draw people strongly to him.

3. Silence

Closely related to not revealing a lot about oneself is not saying too much, period. Why? Again, that keeps people wondering about them. You've no doubt been acquainted with someone who doesn't talk very much, no matter the situation. You're not necessarily drawn to them *per se*. However, if they ever approach you to tell you something, your level of intrigue would go up more than it normally would have, even without knowing what it is they are going to tell you about. If that person has value to you, your intrigue increases that much more.

Why is Brevity Attractive?

So, why is brevity so attractive? Naturally, our brains like to fill in gaps. If there is an unknown variable about something that is relevant to your life, your brain wants to explore and understand it. Your brain goes into a loop of curiosity, drawing and refuting conclusions, until it finally gets a definitive answer. This organ never wants to feel *incomplete* or *lacking*.

Our brains do the same thing with people who demonstrate brevity. They are demonstrating many gaps to be filled. This naturally draws others powerfully to them because our brains so desperately want to fill in the gaps. If not filled, they remain in a loop of curiosity, which turns into excitement.

Key Takeaways

➤ Brevity is when a person reveals themselves in small amounts.

➤ Brevity is the spice of life; it is not only attractive but *necessary*.

➤ Our brains love definitive answers and want to fill in the gaps, so we are drawn to those who demonstrate brevity because we are curious about them and want those gaps to be filled.

Chapter 7: Mastery

What is Mastery?

Naturally, the first thought that comes to mind when one hears the word "mastery" is perfection. Mastery does not equate to perfection. Instead, mastery is about reaching a level of such competency that your ability to gain repeated success becomes easy. Usually, this appears in one major domain within a person's life. However, this can also include refined individuals, which I'll talk about later in the chapter.

What Does Mastery Look Like?

Michael Jordan and Mother Theresa are two names I mentioned earlier in the book. I'll throw a few more into the mix: Mohammed Ali, Tiger Woods, Michael Jackson, Leonardo da Vinci, and Beyoncé. All of these people have dedicated their lives to a domain which they mastered. They reached such heights in their respective fields that their expertise is still felt and admired by many—and are remembered for their accomplishments. These individuals are (or were) on top of their game. They achieved mastery.

Let's dive deeper into the two examples from Chapter 1: Mother Theresa and Michael Jordan.

More than likely, when you hear these two names, thoughts of admiration and inspiration come to mind. You are drawn to them. By some chance, if you haven't heard or know much about these two, take someone (globally known) that you highly admire. The same things I'm about to explain will apply to that person as well.

Michael Jordan is widely regarded as the best professional basketball player of all time. He was so good that his fame transcended basketball. His work ethic, dedication, and intense desire towards becoming the best basketball player he could be took him to a level of success that *he* himself didn't expect. His mastery has attracted so many people to such a point that he successfully created a brand. He uses it on shoes and other merchandise. "Jordan's" (AKA Jays) are some of the most popular shoes on the market and are coveted by many people who don't even play basketball! In fact, people have been known to lose their lives over his brand of shoes, even though the shoes themselves are not the best quality shoes known to man. They are highly sought after because it's the attraction to the man that the brand represents. Michael Jordan represents so well the idea of mastery (which, as you're learning, is one of the eight major aspects of attraction).

From a completely different sphere of life, the late Mother Theresa's name is synonymous with selfless giving. Mother Theresa is best known for being the image of caring for the poorest and most unfortunate. She dedicated her life to serving them as best as she could, going above and beyond what was deemed "necessary" by society. Of course, she never tried to become as famous as she is—that is just a testament to her dedication to her work as a nun.

Although she is no longer living, people are still powerfully drawn to this woman because of how she achieved mastery in her domain.

These two individuals are examples of extreme mastery at a global scale.

People can achieve mastery at a much smaller scale, such as the perennial chess champion in high school, the single mother who figured out how to raise her three kids on one salary, the waiter who knows the menu like the back of his hand and never needs to write any orders down, a globetrotter who has traveled to many countries and encountered many different cultures, a person who has been on a job for 20 plus years and has "been there and done that," the entrepreneur who has mastered the art of closing business deals, and so on. The list is endless.

Anyone who has put in effort in an area of their life to the point where achieving replicable success has become easy for them in that particular domain has mastery. This is highly attractive.

It is most salient when their mastery is found in their life's purpose.

Mastery in the Sense of Being Refined

Earlier, I mentioned that refined individuals can also be categorized as having achieved mastery. When I say "refined," I am referring to someone who has been through enough life experiences to the point where they have achieved a certain level of competency in their general life.

The word "refined" gives us a sense of improvement and modification. Essentially, those are qualities of a person who has made mistakes and *applied* the corrections to their life, as a whole. Even if a refined individual has not gone through a specific experience, they have enough knowledge from past experiences to navigate themselves toward success. For instance, a refined person might dress better than they otherwise would have in the past because they have a better sense of which types of clothes are fashionable.

Refined people are also conscious of certain destructive bad habits they previously had and consequently changed them.

A big part of refinement also involves doing things in one's life more efficiently and effectively, simply because they have a better understanding of how things work. "Maturity" almost mirrors this. However, where maturity would be understanding what is necessary to do and then doing it, refinement is that *and going a step beyond.* For instance, where maturity is staying calm and not engaging in a pointless argument with someone, refinement is not only calmly refraining from arguing, but using that person's point of view to gain insight as to how they think, in order to better communicate with them in the future. This type of advanced foresight is difficult to attain. That's why people are drawn to those who are refined. They are the ones most sought out to be leaders in societies.

Age

Most of the time, age correlates to mastery.

The older you are, the more likely you are to achieve mastery. Typically, people who are older have gone through a multitude of life experiences and (in theory) have acquired wisdom through them. This isn't always the case, though. Where refinement is concerned, there are some 18-year-olds who are more refined than some 40-year-olds. That said, with *age* along with *position* elicits a certain expected level of mastery.

In almost every society, it is *expected* that the older you are, the more refined you should be. When that expectation is not met, it's actually seen as unattractive. For instance, people expect that a 40-year-old would be significantly more refined than an 18-year-old. Call that the status quo. The more refined the 40-year-old is compared to the 18-year-old *past* the "status quo," the more attractive they are. Now, if the 18-year-old was refined to the same degree as the 40-year-old, they are automatically *more* attractive than the 40-year-old. Furthermore, if our 40-year-old is *only* refined to the point as the 18-year-old, they are seen as unattractive.

What is that exact amount of refinement a 40-year-old *should* have? Again, it's all in an individual's perception.

Position

Earlier, I touched on position. In almost every society, it is expected that the more influential your position is within the society, the more refined you should be.

For instance, in most Western societies, a 45-year-old university professor would be *expected* to be more refined as an overall person than a 50-year-old rookie stand-up comic. Even though the former is slightly younger than the latter, by and large, the expectation of refinement is higher on the professor. The reason for this is because the widespread perception (within most Western societies) is that a university professor is expected to carry themselves with a high level of refinement, given the nature of their job. In contrast, a stand-up comedian makes a career out of actually doing the opposite. Therefore, despite age, within this context, the younger individual is *expected* to be more refined than the older individual.

Which positions are more influential than others? Although there are positions universally recognized as having more influence than others, as usual, it comes down to perception.

Often, individuals who are masters of their craft automatically have a few of the other factors of attraction, which makes them *more* attractive. They will have a level of certainty and poise with how they approach things.

Complements to Mastery

Personally, I pride myself for consistently maintaining a healthy diet. Of course, like most people, I do still enjoy indulging in pastries and treats. Once in a while, I'll enjoy a few slices of cake. My mouth is watering just thinking about it. Now, the cake on its own would do the trick for me. However, if you add just the right quantity and type of icing, my taste buds don't know what to do with themselves. If, in addition, just the right quantity and type of filling is added on the inside of the cake, game over!

Just as the icing and filling complement the already tempting pastry, there are certain things that complement mastery. Although they are not necessary, these things will take it over the top and enhance an already attractive person.

The "icing and filling" of mastery are: *a straight posture* and *dressing sharply*. The former simply means keeping your back completely straight when walking, when seated, and when interacting with others. The latter is more subjective and essentially equates to dressing up or wearing fancy clothing. This is where your clothes stand out but are still appropriate for the context in which you find yourself. A suit is a good example of such type of clothing. If you add a straight posture and dressing sharply to an already established perception of mastery, the effect is unbelievable. Your level of attractiveness will soar!

Why is Mastery Attractive?

Why is mastery highly attractive? It goes back to the association of reliability and stability our brains make about such individuals (which I explained in depth in Chapter 3). Our subconscious minds scream "reliable" and "must follow" when we encounter those types of people in our lives. This is magnified if the person displays mastery in a domain that we are involved or interested in. That's why those who enjoy hockey are highly drawn to professional hockey players (who they perceive have achieved mastery in hockey). It is also why musicians become popular; they draw people in based on the perception that they've achieved mastery within their craft of music-making.

I'm sure you've seen the following situation at some point in your life, in some way, shape, or form:

Someone received no attention or adoration from others, and were seen as inferior. Then, almost out of nowhere, that person achieved some great feat. Suddenly, the same people who initially gave little attention or adoration are now doing the opposite. This all-too-familiar situation is the result of being drawn in by mastery. Others now *perceive* this person as having reached that level. To the brain, they have *now* become reliable and necessary to follow.

Whether the situation involves one person or a collection of people like a sports team, this happens all the time. Within a sports context, it is known as "joining the bandwagon." As I talked about in Chapter 1, attraction is all about feelings, which can come and go, like the wind. As soon as the perception of mastery is gone, so is the attraction. Of course, this is also the case with the seven other factors of attraction.

Key Takeaways

> ➢ Mastery is about reaching a level of such competency that your ability to gain repeated success becomes easy.
> ➢ Refinement in general life is also a form of mastery.
> ➢ Our brains deem mastery as highly attractive because the brain closely associates it with reliability and stability.

JUSTIN CLOTTEY

Chapter 8: Lightheartedness

"Easygoing," "agreeable," and "unassuming" are a few words that describe those who display lightheartedness. They are the people who you would describe as being pleasant to be around; those you would refer to as "nice."

Lightheartedness can be displayed in a loud, in-your-face type of way or a calmer, subtler one. It is one of the more interesting aspects of attraction because it is the factor with the greatest polarizing effects.

If there is too much or too little, others will get very turned off. Therefore, it truly must be displayed in the proper amount. If it's done just right, its power to attract is unbelievable.

Like most of the others, there are nuances to unpack to really understand how lightheartedness works.

Let's explore them.

What Does Lightheartedness Look Like?

Lightheartedness can be broken down into three elements:
1. Humor
2. Humility
3. Sensitivity

1. Humor

At face value, humor refers to the ability to joke around and make others laugh. However, it is more profound than that. At the root of it, humor involves being able to take a situation and twist it in a way that causes it to appear purposely awkward. Essentially, humor's real effect comes from taking the seriousness out of an otherwise serious or straightforward situation. This is fun and exciting. It's no surprise that people are drawn to this.

Being able to poke fun at others and situations, in an entertaining way, is highly attractive. The ability to poke fun at yourself and not take what you do too seriously can have just as good or an even greater effect. I'll explain why later in the chapter.

Humor can almost be considered an art form. In fact, as I'm sure you're aware, there are people who have made a career out of it. Famous stand-up comics have mastered it—the delivery, the tone, understanding which type of humor their audience will best respond to, and so on. To a lesser degree, people insert humor into their daily conversations *all the time* (whether intentionally or not). In fact, if you've been paying attention, I've even sprinkled humor into different parts of this book!

While we're on the idea of "sprinkling," there is something important to note with humor. Much like with brevity, humor is more effective when it is like the "spice" to the meat. It's best sprinkled in. In other words, when there is already perceived value (outside of someone being funny) and they use humor in their interactions, it enhances their attractiveness.

However, when there is "more spice than meat", so to speak, humor has a negative effect. I'll give you an example of what I mean by using Jim Carrey (actor, comedian, writer, producer, author, and artist).

Carrey is someone primarily known for being funny, causing lighthearted laughter and amusement. A well-known Hollywood personality like him fits the description of humor perfectly. He is highly attractive to many people, but only to a point—because he is almost *exclusively* known for being funny. Consequently, many people don't take him seriously outside the realm of comedy.

2. Humility

People are highly attracted to those who display the right amount of humility—those who put the needs of others ahead of their own and are not afraid to be vulnerable. Such people are neither demanding nor forceful. They seek the betterment of the collective, rather than their own individual comfort, and don't purposefully magnify themselves. This quality is especially attractive when they have a very valid reason to bring attention to themselves but choose not to do so.

A person with a good level of humility is able to take a step back and be thankful for what they have. They are more appreciative of the little things. This leads to optimism and contentment.

People yearn to be around humble people because they bring peace and harmony to situations—an attractive quality.

3. Sensitivity

People who are sensitive to the needs and empathetic to the feelings of others are highly attractive. They are non-judgemental and accepting of others and their flaws. They are primarily concerned with the feelings of others, regardless of how it affects their own self-image. Others feel safe to express themselves to sensitive people and are comforted by them.

Mother Theresa is probably the best world-famous person as an example (as I described in the previous chapter).

What is Outside the Zone of "Just Right"?

For all three elements of lightheartedness, there is what I call a zone of "just right."

This zone could actually apply to all eight aspects of attraction but I exclusively discuss it here because it is the factor with the greatest polarizing effect (which I mentioned at the beginning of this chapter). Again, if there is too much, people will be turned off. Too little elicits the same result. I'll explain just what I mean here.

To highlight what "too little" lightheartedness looks like, let's revisit what was discussed in Chapter 3, the chapter on certainty.

I stated that there is a fine line between certainty and arrogance. Too little lightheartedness has quite the same effect as arrogance. People are uncomfortable around those who are selfish and only look after their own needs. They put their walls up. They will blatantly state their disdain for that kind of person they meet. The feeling that a person is *too* intense is another consequence of a person having too little lightheartedness. It is another way people become uncomfortable. Both of these are obvious and are easily explained.

The Three Repulsion Effects

Less obvious are the repulsion effects of the flip side to the "lightheartedness" coin. They occur when someone displays too much sensitivity, humility, and even humor. That side of the equation is much harder for people to understand.

Luckily for you, I'll be breaking it down here.

Whenever a person displays "too much" lightheartedness, it causes any combination of three things to happen, which are all major turn-offs to others.

The first possibility is scaring people off. I refer to the second as "the path of least resistance" effect. The third is what I call the "forced reciprocation" effect.

1) Scaring People Off

To explain this, I'll give you an illustration using our friend, Miguel, from Chapter 3.

Miguel is at a carnival in Brazil. He is going back home to Holland the next day. He is down to his last €100 and wants to avoid spending his money on unnecessary expenses so he can have money to spend on unforeseen ones that may come up before his flight back to the Netherlands. Therefore, on his way back to his hostel, he will avoid buying the backpack that the local kids are trying to sell him. He'll be very mindful to not even walk in their vicinity. He'll also be on high alert of the many pickpockets around.

Let's say a person from a street corner approached Miguel. After hearing about his predicament from the Dutch traveller himself, the stranger offered to give Miguel a ride to his hostel for free. In addition, he would give Miguel €5000 when they arrived. The stranger goes on to say that he noticed our Dutch friend's shoes are dirty and that he would make a quick trip to the store to buy some shoe shiner and then clean Miguel shoes. Throughout their whole interaction, the stranger never once stopped smiling.

Now, I'm sure if you were in Miguel's shoes (no pun intended), you would rather take your chances walking home than taking advantage of the stranger's kindness (especially being in unfamiliar territory). Instead of helping, he is stressing our tourist friend out with how *overly* sensitive he's being to the situation.

The stranger's kindness could also be perceived as a weakness (as the saying goes), because it gives off the impression that he is actually needy through trying too hard to please. This will make Miguel's brain associate the stranger with uncertainty. If you remember from Chapter 3, the brain is repulsed by uncertainty. This is the opposite of reliability (which is what Miguel needs in this situation). Either way, the stranger is actually repulsing Miguel instead of attracting him because he is so "over the top."

2) The "Path of Least Resistance" Effect

I'm sure you've heard the phrase "Nice guys (and girls) finish last." This a result of the path of least resistance effect. Those who primarily display too much sensitivity and humility are perceived as easy targets for disrespectful treatment. Because they are too agreeable and easygoing, they put up less resistance to demands placed on them, compared to others. People have, subconsciously and consciously, little to no respect for others like that. They are perceived as dispensable, like a candy wrapper.

Let me give a common example to highlight this. Greg has a cousin who is irresponsible and refuses to find a job. In contrast, Greg works very hard for his money. When this cousin wants to buy something, she will always ask Greg for money. Nani (the cousin) knows if she goes to ask her mother, grandfather, father, or brother, they will *all* tell her "No" and "to get a job."

Greg is different.

Greg always tells her to "Try to get a job soon" but reluctantly gives her money anyway. He is overly empathetic toward his cousin and doesn't want to see her struggle. He really doesn't want to continue giving to her, but he feels the need to be overly sensitive to her situation. Greg is enabling her and causing her to walk all over him.

Nani knows her behavior is disrespectful to her cousin, but she doesn't care.

Compared to her other family members (and going through the process of finding a job), Greg is the path of *least* resistance to getting money. Although he thinks he's doing the respectable thing and desires reciprocated respect, to Nani, he is simply an easy target. Even though she may not say it verbally, her actions suggest this.

3) The "Forced Reciprocation" Effect

People *hate* feeling obligated to do something they have no intrinsic desire to do, and will try to avoid it at all costs. This is *especially* the case when they see no significant benefit for doing it.

A person who is overly sensitive and humble can put you in a state of feeling guilty if you don't reciprocate whatever it is you're getting from the person. Many times, to reciprocate would mean expending more energy than you want to expend.

What's worse is there's no actual benefit to you, other than making the other person feel appreciated for the sake of political correctness—or to alleviate the "guilt." Therefore, because of this repulsion, you will try avoiding such people altogether. This is also why a person perceived as needy is such a turn-off.

If you've ever had an overly sensitive or humble family member or co-worker approach you, knowing that they will ask you more questions about your life than you're willing to answer (out of genuine care, of course), you've experienced the forced reciprocation effect.

Why is Lightheartedness so Attractive?

The brain hates to be overly burdened, stressed, or taxed.

As I alluded to earlier, it will do whatever it takes to get you away from any source potential stress (that it deems as unnecessary). Any time your body has to go into a stressful situation that is taxing to your nervous system, it has to then spend energy on keeping you on high alert. This means there is less energy available to put into other more important functions to keep you alive.

Consequently, your brain will draw you to those who present the "right amount" of lightheartedness I described in this chapter, because they create an environment where your brain feels the opposite! It associates them with low stress as well as relievers of tension.

If your brain perceives that a person has too much lightheartedness: (1) it feels overwhelmed, which causes a person to get scared or "creeped out;" (2) it feels like it's in a stressed stated as a result of the forced reciprocation effect; and/or (3) it associates that person as having very little strength and reliability. As you learned earlier, the brain craves sources of strength and reliability. On the flip side, if it perceives a person as having too little lightheartedness, the brain will feel threatened, urge you to put up your walls, and go into "defense mode." Either way, the brain is repelled to the two extremes but strongly drawn to the happy medium. How do we know where the happy medium is? As usual, it comes down to individual perception.

Key Takeaways

> ➢ Simply put, those who display lightheartedness are pleasant to be around.
> ➢ Lightheartedness has three elements to it: humor, humility, and sensitivity.
> ➢ Our brains are drawn to those who display the "right" amount of lightheartedness because it associates them with low stress and relievers of tension.

Chapter 9: Reputation

A person's reputation is potentially the most uplifting factor in terms of what makes someone attractive because it's one that can be established without even meeting or interacting with a person. Simply put, a reputation is the overall perception or impression of someone, which can take into account the person as a whole or a specific aspect of their life.

The effect of a person's reputation on their attractiveness is often subtle. Many people don't even realize how much it effects how attractive *they are* in the eyes of others (or even how attractive others are in theirs).

How a Reputation is Established

A person's reputation can be established by:

1) What one hears or learns about the person from others.

The credibility of *who* is giving the information or simply a large number of people saying the same thing, are the two factors that will affect this. I'll give you an example. You have no idea who Phil is. Let's say your aunt, your best friend, a stranger you spoke to for fifteen minutes, *and* your significant other all know him well. They *all* tell you about how great of a person they think he is. They *all* don't have one negative thing to say. What's more, they start telling you about his qualities that *you* find attractive. Phil's reputation is now established in your eyes. Without even knowing how he looks like, you are automatically attracted to him. To what *degree* depends on you. Conversely, if all you hear about are his negative qualities from those same people, you will be repelled by him—without knowing how he looks like, having met him, etc.

2) One's own impression of a person from their personal experience with them.

By and large, people form their impression of others based of their first few interactions with the person. Once established, that becomes the light with which a person is viewed.

Depending on the individual, this first impression can be *exceedingly* difficult to change.

For instance, if Marie's impression of Farhana is that she is a snob (based on her first few experiences with her) she will see her as a snob, regardless of what she does in the future. Even if she sees Farhana show qualities like empathy toward someone in a few future encounters with her, Marie will *still* perceive her as a snob who happened to show empathy a few times.

If Farhana's impression of Marie is that she is an intellectual, even if Marie does foolish things, Farhana's opinion won't change. In Farhana's eyes, Marie is a very intelligent woman who does foolish things from time to time (as opposed to her being a foolish person all together).

It is entirely possible for a person's reputation to change. However, again, it is often very difficult.

3) A combination of the first two ways.

A person's reputation can also be established by what one hears or learns about the person from others in conjunction with one's own impression of a person from their personal experience with them.

4) By association

A person can develop a reputation in the eyes of someone else, based on the way they perceive *another* person who they are associated with. Those who are more discerning in their assessment of people will tend not to take this route. That said, whether fair or not, it is still a way a person's reputation can be established—either positively or negatively. Let's look at examples that illustrate this.

Example 1: Both of Khalid's parents went to Harvard. They are both very intelligent people. By association, Khalid will have a reputation of being intelligent in the eyes of some. This is an example of a positive association.

Example 2: Jerome has a hot temper. In fact, all of the other people he knows with red hair (like himself) have hot tempers. Jerome finds a redheaded woman he is really drawn to. He decides not to give her a chance because he feels that, as someone with red hair, she *likely* has a hot temper. He knows such a person would not counterbalance him well within a romantic relationship. Therefore, Jerome decides to not pursue her romantically. He made this decision even though she has never shown any signs of having a temper within any of their interactions. This is an example of a negative association.

Why Reputations Form the Way They Do

Now that have I explained *how* reputations are formed, I want to explain *why* they form the way they do and highlight just how powerful it is.

Biases are a key ingredient to why impressions and perceptions are formed. The reputation a person has is always influenced by the personal biases of others, which are often established long before they've even met the person. To highlight the power of biases, I'm going to use the best example any person explaining something to someone else could use: the learner.

Because I will be using you, I'll need you to do some self-reflecting in the next section.

If you've read all the chapters thoroughly up to this point, you will have noticed the recurring names that I've used in examples throughout the book. This was done on purpose, to help you form an image of each person. As you've read, whether aware of it or not, you formed an opinion of each, even from just their names. You met all of them for the first time in Chapter 3. I want you to take a step back and examine some of the main ones.

Here's a quick refresher:

- Farhana was the very certain speaker.
- Marie was the speaker who wasn't very certain.
- Jarvis was the "certain" basketball player from New Orleans who took trips to the unnamed developing country and England.
- Miguel was the Dutch person who tried to prove to Talib that world was round. He was also down to his last €100 on the last day of his trip in Brazil.
- The mysterious Talib, who works as an engineer, argued emphatically against Miguel that the Earth is flat.

Now, take a minute to critically analyze your own opinions about these individuals, however subtle or insignificant. Go through each one and examine the image you had formed of each in your head, just based on the above information. Think about their personalities, their skin color, their race, their hair color, their height, their build, the way they talk, the way they move, how they dress, whether they are soft-spoken, etc. You formed all of these, mostly subconsciously, based on people you know with similar names, who've done similar things, been in similar situations, etc. In other words, your image for each character was formed based on your biases.

Furthermore, through your biases, you established their respective reputations. Now, however subtle, you are drawn to or repelled by the person. To which degree you are attracted to them depends on you.

Now, here's where it gets interesting. I'm going to give you more insight into these people. This new insight will either confirm or change the reputation of each that is in your head. Consequently, you will either become more attracted or less attracted. Keep in mind that this is all done at a subtle level. So, you really have to critically think about it to notice it.

First of all, I want to let you know that some or all of these people *may* be actual people. I'm choosing not to reveal that information. I will, however, give you more details about each person. As you learn the new information, I want you examine what it does to the image you have in your head of the person.

Farhana had a cocaine addiction for much of her life. It caused her to go to jail and steal money from whomever she could easily target.

Talib is an immigrant to America from Nigeria.

Jarvis is autistic.

One year, Marie decided to use her entire bank account savings to travel the world.

Miguel's parents immigrated to the Netherlands from their difficult living situation in Venezuela.

Consequently, he was raised as a Dutch citizen. He speaks fluent Dutch, Spanish, English, Portuguese, and Mandarin.

Step back again. Have your perceptions of each changed? If so, how? Subtly? Significantly? In light of this new information, does how they've been presented throughout the book make them more attractive to you or less so?

If you didn't have an appreciation for the power of reputation before (in terms of how and why it is formed), you do now. These are descriptions of people on a page in a book, whom you will never meet. Just imagine how much more powerful it is when dealing with people you *actually* met or will meet in your life!

One's reputation can be the biggest boost (or killer) of attraction there is. Being aware of it, how it forms, and how to influence it are very important to maximizing attraction. I will give more detail as to how to do that, once you reach the Master's Degree Program section.

Why Does Reputation Attract or Repel so Strongly?

As with every other aspect of attraction, it comes down to how the brain works. Our brains like to be efficient, only wanting to expend energy where it deems it is absolutely necessary. To not waste time or energy, they will make quick associations. In other words, if a situation played out a particular way and elicited a specific outcome, the brain will associate any future similar situations to that outcome. It won't waste effort trying to discern whether or not the outcome *might* be different. If the brain deemed the result favorable, it will draw you to it. If the outcome was negative, the brain will repel you from it. It does the very same with people. The more times the brain sees the same outcome from similar situations, the stronger it will form the bias.

Key Takeaways

> ➤ A reputation is the overall perception or impression of another, which can take into account the person as a whole or a specific aspect of their life.

> ➤ Someone's reputation is established either by what you learn about someone else, your own personal experience with them, or a combination of the two, and is influenced by your biases.

> ➤ Our brains use reputations to be more efficient in our evaluation of people, as they hate expending more energy than necessary (as they would have to if they were to take time to critically analyze every individual in a vacuum).

Chapter 10: Physical Appearance

The physical features of a person are those that can be seen visually and externally.

One's physical appearance plays a significant role in how attractive someone is perceived to be, and is primarily where romantic and sexual attraction stems from.

People are physically drawn to others based on five factors:
1. Facial features
2. Build
3. Height
4. Dress/Style
5. Color

It is important to note that everyone ranks the five differently. Also, every person has their own preferences, where the nuances of each of the five are concerned.

There are three lenses through which we will examine the each of the five factors:
1) In a general sense
2) Those physically drawn to males
3) Those physically drawn to females

It is important to note that what is described here applies *for the vast majority of people* but is *in no way* absolute. There will always be exceptions to any rule.

1. Facial Features

Facial features are all the parts of the face and how they are positioned in relation to each other: eyes, eyebrows, nose, ears, lips, jaw, head shape, chin, forehead, facial hair, and teeth.

1) In a General Sense

From an objective and general standpoint, the types of faces that are most attractive are those with symmetrical features.

I touched on this in Chapter 5 and explained how it's the balance that is appealing.

Furthermore, the brain associates symmetrical facial features with being healthy.

2) Those Physically Drawn to Males

Those drawn (romantically or sexually) to males will find facial features that show strength, maturity, and refinement more attractive.

Such features would be (but aren't limited to):
- A well-defined jawline, with more of a square shape
- Facial hair
- A mature-looking face
- A protruding chin

Note: Scars, having a deep voice, and displaying neutral facial expressions in day-to-day interactions are a few of the things that contribute to the attractiveness of a male face.

3) Those Physically Drawn to Females

Those drawn (romantically or sexually) to females will find facial features that display youthful vibrancy and vitality more attractive.

Such features would be (but aren't limited to):
- Bright, wide eyes (irises and pupils)
- Rounded faces
- Dimples
- Smooth, elastic, and healthy skin on the face (and no facial hair)
- Symmetrical proportions between eyes, eyebrows, nose, and mouth

Note: Things like silky flowing hair, a higher-pitched voice/laugh, and facial expressions that are innocent and inviting (like joyful smiling) are few things that contribute to the attractiveness of a female face.

Remember, not all of the listed features are necessary for attraction (whether male or female). Sometimes, just a combination of a few will suffice.

The variations and the nuances of which features are more attractive over others varies from person to person.

2. Build

This is the size and shape of a person's body.

1) In a General Sense

From an objective and general standpoint, the most attractive bodies are ones where the limbs and torso are well-proportioned (balanced), with little to no visible deformities. There are many types of builds that different people find attractive. If you recall, in Chapter 5, I discussed how fit bodies best demonstrate an attractive build. A body that's "in shape" suggests other important qualities for person to have, such as discipline, health, etc.

2) Those Physically Drawn to Males

Those drawn (romantically or sexually) to males will find builds that show strength and durability to be more attractive.

Such aspects would be (but aren't limited to):
- A large, wide frame
- Well-defined muscles

A typical type of attractive male body is one where the shoulders and chest are broad, the torso is strong and tapering, abdominal muscles are visible, and arms are muscular or strong-looking, all accompanied by strong legs that are proportionate to the upper body.

Interestingly enough, male bodies that are on the pudgier side can be very attractive to those attracted to males. On the surface, this is completely counterintuitive but this type of body is an association to an older, mature male (father-like figure) on a subconscious level. I explain this more in the next chapter. These types of bodies are often referred to in popular Western culture as "dad bods."

3) Those Physically Drawn to Females

Those drawn (romantically or sexually) to females will find builds that show more vitality and health (with less of a focus on pure strength) more attractive. Furthermore, specifically where the female body is concerned, there is more of an emphasis on childbearing potential.

Such aspects would be (but aren't limited to):

- The hip-to-waist ratio (thinner waist with wider hips)
- The proportion of cleavage size relative to the rest of the body (the better proportionated, the more attractive)
- The gluteal musculature accompanied by a certain amount of fat in the region
- Proportionate size and length of legs in relation to the upper body

3. Height

This is how tall a person is.

1) In a General Sense

In a generally sense, the taller someone is the more attractive they are. However, the general perception of an "ideal height" differs between males and females.

2) Those Physically Drawn to Males

Those drawn (romantically or sexually) to males, by and large, will find those who are taller than them to be *more* attractive. In fact, heightwise, the taller the male, the stronger the attraction. A tall structure subconsciously gives the perception of being better suited to protect and lead, which we discuss in Chapter 11.

3) Those Physically Drawn to Females

Those drawn (romantically or sexually) to females will typically find those who are shorter or around the same height as *more* attractive. There is less of a universally perceived *ideal* height for females as compared to males.

4. Dress/Style

This is how a person puts themselves together, from the hairstyles and types of clothing they wear to any piercings and/or tattoos they might have. This is the easiest of the five physical features one can alter or change.

1) In a General Sense

From an objective and general standpoint, the appeal in the way a person dresses and styles themselves is extremely diverse. That said, the one thing that is consistently considered *unattractive* is dressing "inappropriately" within a given context one finds themselves in (i.e., dressing in a swimming suit at a formal wedding ceremony in a church).

2) Those Physically Drawn to Males

Those drawn (romantically or sexually) to males will find those who style themselves in a way that displays their strength and authority *more* attractive—for example, someone who has a muscular physique dresses in clothing that make their muscles stand out or those who wear clothing that displays their authority in a field (i.e., a uniform, a suit, etc.).

3) Those Physically Drawn to Females

Those drawn (romantically or sexually) to females will find those who style themselves in a way that accentuates their physical features more to be *more* attractive—for example, those who wear clothing like tight-fitting pants, form-fitting shirts, etc.

5. Color

This encompasses a person's skin color/shade (how light or dark they are), eye color, and hair color. Of course, this speaks to more societal constructs where color is concerned (like race).

1) In a General Sense

In terms of what is attractive from an objective and general standpoint, color is the hardest to nail down. Where attraction is concerned, there are many kinds of preferences as to the color of these various features.

When race is taken into account, different factors of attraction come into play, such as balance (see

Chapter 5) and reputation (see Chapter 9), to name a few.

Those Physically Drawn to Males and Those Physically Drawn to Females

When discussing what draws those who are romantically or sexually drawn to males and females, it is much the same as what I previously mentioned. There are too many variables.

An Important Note about All Five Aspects

It goes without saying that all five features must be complemented by external factors (such as having good hygiene) to maximize physical attractiveness.

Why Physical Appearance is Attractive

To fully grasp how physical features are perceived as attractive, it is important have an understanding of "masculine" and "feminine" energy, where they come from, and why humans have been hardwired the way they have been for thousands of years. I will be explaining these things in the next chapter.

Key Takeaways

> ➤ The physical features of a person are those that can be seen visually and externally. They primarily come into play with romantic and sexual attraction.

> The five aspects of a person's physical features are their facial features, build, height, dress/style, and color.

> From a romantic attraction standpoint, which exact physical features are perceived as more or less attractive is predicated on which type of energy a person is drawn more to ("masculine" or "feminine").

JUSTIN CLOTTEY

Chapter 11: Romantic Attraction

Romantic attraction and sexual attraction are terms that can be—and often are—used interchangeably. However, romantic attraction usually results in sexual attraction but sexual attraction doesn't always result in romantic attraction. It's like squares and rectangles. All squares are rectangles but not all rectangles are squares. (Hopefully, the first time you learned this was in elementary school math class and not from a book on attraction.)

When one is romantically attracted to someone, they are consequently sexually attracted to the person. They will desire having sexual relations with the person (assuming all the appropriate factors lined up). The "appropriate factors" vary from person to person. For instance, if they were in a committed relationship (perhaps only in marriage), they were both single, they had the opportunity to be alone together, etc.).

On the other hand, if someone is sexually attracted to someone, that doesn't necessarily mean they will be romantically attracted because romantic attraction suggests more of a desire of a type of exclusive and intimate relationship. This type of attraction will almost always take into consideration the eight factors, although which particular ones will depend on the individual.

There is often a huge disconnect between partners within a romantic relationship context. This is the result primarily, I believe, of a lack of understanding of how people's energies work.

In order to fully understand how romantic and sexual attraction work, you must understand masculine energy and feminine energy. A significant amount of sexual and romantic attraction between people come from the balancing of the two energies. The next logical questions are: What are they? Where do they come from?

I'll explain, because here's where it gets really interesting, but before I continue, I want to make something very clear. It is important when reading through this section, to *not* get caught up in genders per se. The focus should be more on the energies *themselves*. Every time you read "masculine energy," the temptation will be to filter what I'm saying through your idea of men, with the same happening with feminine energy and your idea of women. Keep in mind, some people don't even self-identify as male or female. *Everyone, irrespective* of who they are, has a combination of both energies. With that out of the way, I will proceed.

Masculine and Feminine Energies

What exactly are masculine and feminine energies? They describe the two types of polarizing "urges" to perform certain behaviors that exist in all humans. Like I said, every human (regardless of sexual orientation or gender) has both. However, each person will default to one of the two energies more often than not. That is a consequence of them being more comfortable in that energy because of their biological makeup and the social environment they were raised in. Thus, it is a combination of nature and nurture.

Simply put, masculine energy is the urge to build, compete, and impose one's will, creating rigid structure, direction, purpose, and idealism. In contrast, feminine energy is the urge to be nurturing, warm, emotionally sensitive, yielding, and receptive, as well as to make connections with others.

Let me explain this further using an illustration of a car trip from Point A to Point B.

Masculine energy looks like: planning the car trip with the objective to strictly move from Point A to Point B, making sure there's gas in the tank, spare tires in the trunk, the routes are mapped out on a physical map (just in case the GPS malfunctions), and anticipating potential detours to overcome. The focus is on being self-reliant and hashing out all the necessary details to make the trip more efficient. The plan is well-thought-out and rigid, moving from Point A to Point B with as minimal disruptions as possible.

Feminine energy looks like: moving from Point A to Point B is the main plan. However, along the way, if there is a need to take a detour, so be it. Although the necessities of the trip will be accounted for, there's more of a focus on making adjustments when and as needed. There's room for amendments, depending on the *sense* or *feeling* within a given moment. A rigid plan won't allow room for this. The main objective is to get from Point A to Point B following the initial plan. *However*, there's enough leeway so that at any given moment along the way, if something unexpected arises to help or improve the situation, plans are liable to change.

The naming of the masculine and feminine energies is very curious indeed. The temptation is to associate masculine energy with males and feminine energy with females, but it's certainly more complex than that. As I stated earlier, every person has both energies in them. In order to live life effectively, one must be able to behave in *both* the ways described in the aforementioned example. However, depending on their life situation and how their biology is set up, people will typically find themselves more comfortable behaving (whether through comfort or necessity) more in one energy than another. For instance, those who have been thrust into life situations where quick, decisive behavior is necessary for survival (such as is common with children raised living conditions with high poverty and crime) will typically default to masculine energy (irrespective of gender) in every context, almost exclusively.

So, why call one energy masculine and the other feminine? By and large, the naming is because men (those with male physical features) are biologically predisposed to having more masculine energy. Conversely, women (those with female physical features) are biologically predisposed to having more feminine energy. This is the result of the presence of hormones as well as biological hardwiring over thousands of years.

Testosterone and Estrogen

Although everyone has both types of hormones, those with male bodies typically have significantly more testosterone in their bodies and those with female bodies typically have significantly more estrogen in their bodies. The prevalence of these hormones not only affects our physical makeup but how we behave and think as well. This is where the hardwiring comes into play, as you'll see in a moment.

Testosterone is primarily responsible for most men being naturally physically bigger and stronger than most women. It is also the primary reason for the facial hair and body shape they develop (see Chapter 10). Testosterone is also responsible for increasing the urge for aggressive behavior and having a high sex drive. The more one has, the more all of these are magnified.

Some women are born with more testosterone naturally occurring in their bodies than the "average range" for women. Consequently, they will have more of an "urge" for what I just described and will tend to naturally be more comfortable within their masculine energy. They will also naturally have more musculature with less curviness on their bodies. Conversely, men born with less testosterone than within the "average range" will have a lessened "urge" for aggressive behavior and a lower sex drive. They are also typically more comfortable in their feminine energy.

Now, let's look at the hardwiring side of the equation.

Hardwiring for Partner Selection

Let's go back to the very early days of the human existence, when everything was much more primitive. In those less sophisticated times, one's natural biological makeup influenced their behavior almost exclusively. Also, keep in mind that all the way back then, living conditions were very harsh and the options for finding others to engage in a sexual relationship with were scarce. Therefore, it increased the urgency of finding a suitable person one could enter a sexual relationship with. As a result, the sexual relationships in that time were almost exclusively for procreation purposes. Consequently, sexual activity had significantly fewer rules and negative stigmas associated with it than in modern history. With the further development of human societies came the rules surrounding sexual activity.

As a consequence of having significantly more testosterone, the average man was bigger, stronger, and better suited for physical labor than the average women. At the same time, women's biological makeups made them better suited for doing other things (nurturing children and forming deeper emotional connections). With this distinction came set roles that men and women were expected to play, in relation with each other. This was how it was for thousands of years.

Human civilization began to advance because of the realization that collaboration (by creating relationships) was necessary.

These relationships (or partnerships) were created to perpetuate the survival and thriving of all parties involved. Specifically, the relationship role between men and women began to forge. The goal was finding a partner or partners who played roles you were less capable of.

At that time, the primary relationship between men and women was a sexual one, for the purpose of creating offspring, who would perpetuate the survival of the species.

Here is where it gets interesting (if it isn't already). Any man could have a sexual relationship with any woman and vice versa. However, not all sexual relationships would be the *most* beneficial to both parties. The partners that were targeted for sexual relationships were targeted based on what was most beneficial for the man (from his perspective) and most beneficial for the woman (from her perspective).

For thousands of years, this influenced the behavior of males and females in how they evaluated the opposite sex. Consequently, even in modern times, males and females still subconsciously align their behaviors with those deep-seated, habitual patterns.

Males were (and are) able to produce an unlimited amount of their male sex seed (sperm) for their entire lives. Females had (and have) a set limit to how many of their sex seeds (ovum) their bodies produced and for a limited amount of time. As they got (and get) older, the *quality* of those ovum would (and will) lower, which resulted in increased chances of developmental problems for the potential zygote.

The Male's Selection Process

From the testosterone-filled man's perspective, to maximize his chances of having offspring in his limited amount of time on earth:

1) He would *aggressively* look for younger women. This was to increase the probability that she had the maximum amount of ovum that were at their highest quality.

2) He would look for women who looked the most "fertile." Factors like the proportions of her hips and waist (where the child-rearing would directly take place), her gluteal muscle and fat stores around that area (more meant a better support of the child during development), breast size, her own physical fitness, her facial features

being proportionate, and a good quality of her skin (all factors tied to beauty) spoke to her healthiness and the increased probability of successfully being able to rear children.

3) Having a higher sex drive (from testosterone) would push him to engage in as many sexual relations with as women as he could access. Mass producing his sex seed was not an issue, so this engagement was more beneficial to him, overall.

Less important to the man in a woman was her ability to protect him. He would be already be more naturally aggressive and better suited for physical combat than the women he would typically enter a sexual relationship with.

The Female's Selection Process

From the perspective of the less testosterone-filled (and physically weaker) woman, to maximize her chances of having offspring in her limited amount of time on earth, she would seek:

1) The strongest man (physically and emotionally) she could find. As the physically weaker person, she needed the best protection possible, for not only herself but her potential offspring as well. A strong man would be especially necessary during her time of pregnancy (when she was at her most vulnerable). Emotional strength was almost just as important for her because entering a relationship with a man who was not in control of his emotions would lead to more danger.

2) Someone who was older than her. This increased the chances that he would have more wisdom, refinement, and emotional control. This would ensure he would make better decisions, ultimately beneficial to her, as she would be less able to defend herself and her potential offspring during physical turmoil.

3) Someone who could provide for her. She was *less* physically suited to amass major resources (food, materials for building shelters, etc.). Back then, these key resources weren't readily available as they are today. Less important to her was his physical beauty (proportions of facial features, quality of skin, etc.) because it didn't affect his strength, maturity, or ability to amass resources.

Dating Strategies

All the way back then, the woman's strategy for seeking a man was significantly different than the man's. She played a more passive role in the selection process. This was because she couldn't afford to aggressively seek a man. If something went wrong, she would likely be unable to defend herself. Consequently, she relied on the art of subtly and enhancing her physical features to entice men she was interested in to come to her. If a man *didn't* pick up on her signs, she would rather let a "good one" get away than risk aggressively pursuing a "wrong one."

This contrast in "dating strategies" from all the way back in those days is why we see many of the behavioral patterns we see today within the context of finding a suitable partner. *It comes down to the hardwiring from the primitive days.*

When looking to enter a sexual relationship back in the early days, men were *aggressive* in their search for a partner(s). Because of their hardwiring for efficiency, they would streamline their criteria. Men searched for quick clues (i.e., physical features) to help decide whether or not a particular woman was a viable option. Her main value to him was being able to produce healthy offspring. Men were less concerned with her character or how they connected emotionally. They would be the aggressor; they would do the choosing. Consequently, given this dynamic, men would *naturally* assume the leadership role. This explains why *many* modern-day men will tend to continue "pursuing" the same woman over and over, even when she *subtly* tries to let him know she is not interested. In contrast, *many* modern-day women are able to move on a lot more easily from someone who is not interested in them.

By and large, this is the reason the modern-day man is primarily highly attracted to a woman's physical features as well as her nurturing soft side. He is *less* concerned with her ability to provide resources and protection for him. This is why men can light up and "fall in love" so quickly, without really knowing a woman in depth. When they reach this level of romantic attraction, they are ready to jump in very quickly into relationship (often sooner than the woman). This is why it's easier for the modern-day man to reach that level of romantic (and more often sexual) attraction with *many* women at once. They're more simplistic about what attracts them. That makes it *harder* for them to connect deeply on an emotional level. They are hardwired to be more motivated by laying claim to a woman over developing a deep emotional connection with her.

In contrast, where partner selection was concerned, historically speaking, women had more of a focus on the deeper qualities of a man (outside just the physical) because she had less room for error. As a result, women adopted the more passive role in partner selection, preferring to take her time and stay focused on a man's communication and sense of control (of himself, situations, and even others). It wasn't that women would only ever have one sexual partner; it was that they were more selective, compared to men.

This is why, by and large, in order for the modern-day woman to reach a high level of romantic attraction, she takes into consideration many more factors than just a man's physical features. For this reason, it takes her longer to "fall in love," as compared to time it takes for the modern man. The "work" is cut short if a woman sees other women highly attracted to the man. It is why the modern-day woman will examine how other women perceive a man. *This is a strategy the modern-day man relies less on.* Among the factors she is constantly assessing is his strength of character (emotional as well as physical) and his ability to amass resources (things like finances and his ability to influence others). Once at a high level of romantic attraction, less important are the details of a man's physical body. More important to her is a deep emotional connection (sharing things that make them feel more bonded together).

Once she has reached a high level of romantic attraction, it's also why she vehemently wants to establish a committed relationship. In a sense, this is a *claim* on its own, after "in-depth" research. That's why it's hard for the average modern-day woman to reach a *high* level of romantic attraction quickly and for more than one man.

Hardwiring for General Behavior Patterns

Now, keeping all of this as the backdrop, we can understand how behaviors of men and women would be different, not just when searching for sexual partners, which monopolized much of their livelihood, but even in day-to-day behaviors as well.

Men, being more aggressive and better suited for physical activities, constantly hunted for food, engaged in physical combat, built things, and explored. It is the reason why engaging in sports is so thrilling for many men in the modern age— it gives them an opportunity to carry out their intrinsic desire to dominate in physical "warfare" by applying structured strategy (in a safe, socially acceptable manner). This, in essence, is why the urges that are in line with these described types of behaviors are classified as *masculine energy*.

Women, being less aggressive and *more* susceptible to physical danger, were more cautious in their day-to-day behaviors. As I mentioned earlier, they had to master the art of subtly in many of their interactions. Because their biological makeup was designed to carry offspring, they had to develop a heightened sense of cautiousness.

In addition, women had to develop a heightened sense of sensitivity, nurturing, and emotional awareness. The average woman couldn't afford to be idealistic or rigid with her behavior but rather was more practical and open to constant adjustments in her approach to daily life (making them less prone to risk-taking). This, in essence, is why the urges that are in line with these types of behaviors are classified as *feminine energy*.

Nurture

Although I've already touched on the nurture side of the equation, I'm going to highlight a few things. If one was raised in a society where the natural urges (as previously described) that were based on their biological makeup forged a fixed role for them within that society, their behavior would typically be in line with the "traditional" gender roles (i.e., men would behave like men have typically behaved throughout human history, and women would behave like women have typically behaved throughout human history).

Conversely, if the society shames the traditional gender roles, the result is often an unspoken switch to "inversed" gender roles with behaviors that fall in accordance with them (i.e., men would behave like women have typically behaved throughout human history, and women would behave like men have typically behaved throughout human history). Typically, this shaming of the "traditional" gender roles comes as a consequence of men being in an overly dominant and abusive position over women. This (almost unconscious) inverse is done in an effort to tip the scales to a more equitable balance. We see this type of trend in many modern Western societies.

It is important to note that these aren't absolute rules, but objectively observable trends.

Counterbalance and Romantic Attraction

As I stated earlier in the chapter, everyone has both types of energy in them. By and large, within a romantic context, people are *less* attracted to those who display too much of the energy which they are more comfortable in. This shows itself in many ways, which I'll discuss later. Those who are *more* comfortable in their feminine energy, as many women are, are less *romantically* attracted to those who have as much or more feminine energy that they have. Those comfortable in masculine energy, as many men are, are less *romantically* attracted to a similar amount of masculine energy. There must be a *counterbalance.*

Furthermore, it is important to understand that comfort in a particular energy is a range and not a fixed setting. Think of the energies like a dimmer switch as opposed to a light switch. In terms of attraction to the other, the more extreme on the range a person's default comfort is, the more they are attracted to the opposite energy, further into the extreme of its range. The closer one is to the middle of an energy, the more drawn they are to the opposite energy, closer to the middle of the range.

As I warned you about earlier, remember to *not* fall for the association trap of masculine energy with men and feminine energy with women. Some men are more comfortable in feminine energy, while some women are comfortable in masculine energy. In such cases, what I'm explaining here still applies to them as well.

Also, keep in mind that a *romantic* attraction is a specific kind of attraction. Two people with the same energy can still be highly attracted to each other.

Within the context of a monogamous romantic relationship, the probability of the two "drifting apart" increases substantially when partners are constantly in energies that they are not comfortable in. In this situation, partners will look (either consciously or subconsciously) for other potential romantic partners who can better counterbalance their preferred energy. In order to keep the romantic or sexual attraction strong, both parties much remain in the energies they are most comfortable in and be counterbalanced by the opposite energy (at the proper point within the range) of their partner.

There are some theories that the anatomy of the sex organs have evolved to reflect the masculine and feminine dynamic. A specific example is where an outward-pointing penis is meant to be invasive in relation to the vagina, which is yielding and meant to receive and be penetrated by the penis. However, such concepts (whether accurate or not) are beyond the scope of this book but are certainly an interesting complement to what I'm explaining here.

By default, masculine and feminine energies, respectively, cause people to display particular behaviors in line with the eight main factors of attraction. Consequently, through the lens of romantic attraction, people will be drawn stronger toward those who display more of those qualities than others. Keep in mind that *all* of the eight factors of attraction (when displayed within their "proper" proportions) are *extremely* attractive to *everyone*. With that said, from a romantic attraction standpoint, outside of physical features, certainty and mastery are *especially* attractive to those comfortable in feminine energy. Lightheartedness and ease are *especially* attractive to those comfortable in masculine energy. From a hardwiring perspective, the behaviors of someone who embodies certainty and mastery fall directly in line with the strength of character, reliability, and stability aspects that counterbalance the feminine energy. On the other hand, the behaviors of a person who embodies lightheartedness and ease fall directly in line with the sensitivity, agreeableness, and poise that counterbalance the masculine energy.

Something interesting also tends to happen within a romantic relationship context where the counterbalancing of energies is concerned: *People revert to different energies, depending on who they are with.*

Naturally, the partner who shows more masculine energy (regardless of gender) will cause their partner to move more into their feminine energy. This is because the masculine energy (as explained earlier) is more of the assertive/leadership energy, while the feminine energy is pliable and yielding. In fact, this happens even outside of a romantic context. It happens among friends, strangers, in a business setting, etc.

To illustrate this, we'll bring back Farhana (from the previous chapter).

Naturally, Farhana is *more* comfortable in her feminine energy. However, she is more comfortable in her masculine energy than her boyfriend is in his. Consequently, when they are together, her boyfriend reverts to his feminine energy when he is around her.

In contrast, Farhana's friend, John, is naturally *more* comfortable in his masculine energy than she is. So, when *those* two are together, Farhana reverts to her feminine energy because John displays more masculine energy than her.

What then tends to happen, given this phenomenon, is that there is a drop in romantic attraction for their partner when one (or both) are constantly operating from the energy they are not comfortable in.

It's important to understand that neither energy is inherently better than the other. Like I mentioned earlier, both are necessary to live a successful and fruitful life.

Furthermore, if you really step back and observe it, the proverbial "dance" between the two is incredibly beautiful.

We can fast forward to present day.

These energies (and behaviors, by extension) have been so deeply hardwired into the human brain from many thousands of years of the same patterns. This is why, by and large, men and women think and behave in accordance with the behaviors of very long ago (especially within a romantic context).

Understanding the Friend Zone

A popular concept in Western society is termed the "friend zone." It is a very common yet confusing phenomena for many people who are undereducated in romantic relationship dynamics—whether you are the person "being put" in the friend zone or "putting someone" else in there. In essence, this is when a person does not feel that "spark" with someone and can never consider them as a romantic partner. The person still brings enough value to their life, so they'd still like to keep them as a friend. That "spark" is one of two things.

1) The person in the "friend zone" doesn't display enough (or a specific few) of the eight aspects of attraction (certainty, ease, balance, brevity, mastery, lightheartedness, reputation, and physical appearance) as explained in this book.

2) The person doesn't counterbalance their energy enough (whether masculine or feminine).

Both of these come down to perception. What's enough or the right amount all depends on the individual.

IPOA vs. EPOA

A person's internal perception of their attractiveness (IPOA) and their external perception of attractiveness (EPOA) play a major factor where romantic relationships are concerned. The IPOA is how attractive someone considers themselves. The EPOA is how attractive others perceive them.

More often than not, people allow their EPOA to influence their IPOA (although the two are inherently independent of each other). A legitimate argument can be made that your EPOA is, in fact, more important in attracting the romantic partners than your IPOA.

Together, the IPOA and EPOA also influence a person's perception of the suitable romantic partners for them. There are four combinations that lead to four different mindsets.

Combination #1: High EPOA + High IPOA

Result: From the many options they have available to them, this person is very particular about who they enter a romantic relationship with. They have very high standards.

Combination #2: Low EPOA + High IPOA

Result: This person is pickier, based on *unrealistically* elevated standards.

Combination #3: High EPOA + Low IPOA

Result: This person will have many options (whether suitable or not) but will be less picky.

Combination #4: Low EPOA + Low IPOA

Result: They'll be very open with the limited options available to them.

Of course, there are variations within each. This is just to give you an idea of how people generally think, given their IPOA and EPOA. As I've been talking about since the beginning, attraction is never set in stone; it can be raised or lowered. It is no different with a person's EPOA and IPOA. Throughout out a person's life, these can change as well, depending on different circumstances.

As you've learned throughout this chapter, romantic attraction is nuanced and has many contributing factors to it. After reading this chapter, you should have a firm grasp on how the dynamic works within this type of attraction work and *why* they are like that.

Key Takeaways

> Everyone has masculine energy and feminine energy within them. However, people are more comfortable in one than the other, which will consequently dictate how they behave.

> The way people choose romantic partners is based on the hardwiring of the habitual patterns from their ancestors.

> Masculine and feminine energies need to be counterbalanced within a romantic relationship context.

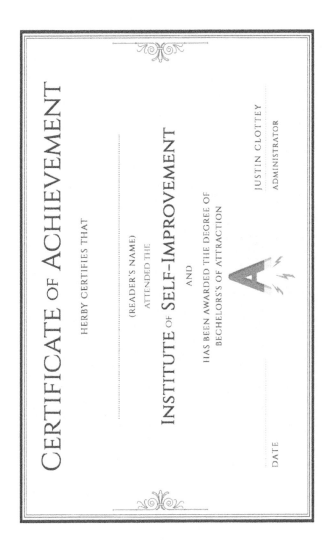

CERTIFICATE OF ACHIEVEMENT

HERBY CERTIFIES THAT

(READER'S NAME)

ATTENDED THE

INSTITUTE OF SELF-IMPROVEMENT

AND

HAS BEEN AWARDED THE DEGREE OF
BECHELORS'S OF ATTRACTION

JUSTIN CLOTTEY
ADMINISTRATOR

DATE

SECTION TWO:

MASTER'S DEGREE PROGRAM

Chapter 12: The Guidelines

There's a reason why most Bachelor's Degree programs are designed to be four to five years long, while most Master's Degree programs are no more than two years. The former is supposed to give you the foundation of what you're studying. It is comprehensive so you can really understand the big picture. On the other hand, the latter is designed to be an opportunity for you to *apply* your acquired knowledge in a more specific area. There's more of an emphasis on independently producing something practical, as opposed to learning more theory. The expectation is that you will be able to go out and do your own research to complement or add to what you've learned in your program. Your Master's Degree Program provides you with a framework and a few guidelines. The rest is on you. If you've gone through both types of programs in your life, you understand this.

This book is no different. The "Bachelor's Degree Program" in this book is eleven chapters long. Its main purpose was to give you the foundation on what makes a person attractive. Furthermore, the undertow of that section was to help you gain a clearer understanding of who *you're* drawn to and *why*.

153

In this section of just one chapter, you are expected to *put that knowledge to action* using the given guidelines.

My hope is that you will use the framework given in this "Master's Degree Program" as a guide to find out more about yourself and then build upon it—with the ultimate goal of improving your image in the eyes of others and yourself.

Let's begin.

1. Certainty

1) Become certain by finding out what *you* believe in—not just half-heartedly but what you *fully* believe in. Evaluate what is true and what is untrue to you. Develop a system of processing information and situations and *stick to it.* For that, you really must invest time learning about life principles and how things (and people) work. Reading a book like this is a step in that direction.

2) Find what you're *truly* passionate about. If you have trouble, try out a myriad of things. Don't limit yourself to only specific kinds of experiences. You may have to get out of your comfort zone.

Once you find it, stick to it! Develop it and actively seek out those who can help you do so.

3) *Display* more certainty in your life, particularly in your interactions with others. When you speak, do so with conviction and assuredness. Speak with the same amount of

conviction as you would if you were explaining to someone that two plus two equals four.

4) When you decide to do something, do not hesitate. Just do it. Practice not taking it back. If you feel you might have made a mistake, have enough belief in yourself that you can resolve it. To avoid (further) mistakes, have a firm understanding of the situations (or potential situations) you find yourself in *beforehand*.

How do you develop more belief? Like you learned in the Bachelor's Degree Program, simply *decide* to believe.

5) Become more resilient in your certainty, so that when it is challenged (which it will be), you don't lose your certainty. Focus on body language that gives off an impression of certainty. Specifically, display open body language and maintain an erect posture. Make this a habit, even when you don't feel like it.

6) When doing or saying things, be very clear. Don't beat around the bush. Just do exactly what it is or state it in simple terms.

2. Ease

1) Display more ease in your life by not trying so hard to do something. Be *visibly* calm and in control of your reactions to *anything*. Tamper them down.

2) Invest time in methods that help you consistently relax. Mediation, journaling, quiet

time to reflect, and consistent sleep are a few great methods to use.

3) Keep things simple, all the way down to how you move. Don't expend so much energy when you move or interact with others.

3. Balance

1) Gain an understanding of what balances you by examining your strengths, weakness, likes, and dislikes.

2) Take the time to understand what balances others, specifically those you wish to attract. I mean *really* understand.

Take the time to learn. Then you must apply this knowledge to achieve equalizing balance and counterbalance (romantically, platonically, etc.).

3) When dressing and styling yourself, add as much symmetry as possible to your appearance.

Also, don't dress out of context (whether in everyday dressing or at specific events). There is usually a wide range of what would be "acceptable" within the context. Just don't go past that range (i.e., wearing snow pants and four layers of shirts to a beach on a hot summer day).

4. Brevity

1) Add the spice of brevity to your life. Don't be so readily available for others. By that I mean you should legitimately have *many* things going on; do not purposely ignore others!

2) Diversify your time with various types of individuals and situations—ideally, ones that will help you grow. Spend time with different groups of people, being enriched and enriching them. Work on different projects.

3) When interacting with people, ask more questions so you can learn more about people, rather than sharing information about yourself. When giving information about yourself, always keep it brief. Only elaborate if you are asked to.

4) Make a habit of leaving an interaction on a high note, even if it might be a little awkward.

5. Mastery

1) Identify something you're good at. Improve upon it to the level where replicating success in it becomes second nature. This may take time.

2) Teach it to others who might be interested.

3) Provide services to others in relation to it.

4) Refine yourself. Become competent in *many* areas. Educate yourself in various subjects and competencies. Ideally, choose to invest your time and energy in ones that are directly relevant to your lifestyle, then branch out from there.

For instance, if you spend most of your days in the city interacting with people as a tour guide, learn in-depth about the history of the local neighborhoods before learning about something like wilderness survival tactics.

6. Lightheartedness

1) Occasionally, verbalize that you are not the center of the universe. Consistently verbalize your gratitude for what you have. Get to a place where you truly feel a sense of gratitude and humility of yourself, in relation to everyone else.

2) Occasionally, poke fun at yourself. The key word is *occasionally*.

3) *Occasionally*, make witty remarks about the situation you're in when interacting.

4) Poke fun at others when they poke fun at you. As a rule of thumb, wait for them to start it. Don't poke fun at others first. Also, be okay with it, going along with someone poking fun at you. Exaggerate it, even. Remember to keep it playful; don't take it seriously.

5) Show empathy for others who are going through hard times. Help out wherever you can. Try not to go overboard. If it is not your problem, don't make it your problem.

6) Commend people whenever they do something praiseworthy but try not to go beyond the limit, so as to cause distrust in others.

7) If you are dealing with emotional pain and unforgiveness, you must genuinely seek help to heal. Those unresolved issues (whether you know it or not) will cause you to stay bitter at the world (even in subtle ways). Ultimately, this only hurts you!

7. Reputation

1) Maintain a good general reputation. Don't seek to harm anyone. Look to contribute to the lives of others in a positive manner, not subtract from them. When all is said and done, *that is* the best thing you can do for another person—contribute positively to their lives.

2) Be aware of what your impact is, even in the subtle ways. This will take critical analysis; invest the time. Don't be let it prevent you from living your life but make an effort to be aware of how what you do effects people, even in the little ways.

8. Physical Appearance

1) Improve your physical appearance.

Three of the five elements of physical appearance cannot be changed. However, the other two *can* be significantly altered or improved.

Although you cannot change your height, skin tone, or facial features, you *can* improve your dress/style and how "in shape" your build is.

Things like hygiene and healthy food consumption are also always within your control. Find out how to best improve them and then do so.

2) Make sure you *always* maintain an erect posture and make dressing/styling yourself sharply a habit.

9. Improve Your Romantic Attractiveness

If you wish to attract someone specific, find out which energy they are most comfortable in and focus on maximizing the aspects of attraction that best counterbalances that.

If the person is most comfortable in masculine energy, put special emphasis on displaying ease and lightheartedness.

If a person is most comfortable in feminine energy, put special emphasis on displaying certainty and mastery.

Take Time to Apply

Dedicate time—as much as three months—to really developing these guidelines into lifestyle habits. As I mentioned earlier, you actually need to apply them for there to be any type of change. In addition, you must go out and learn more, to supplement the knowledge. It might be messy and awkward, especially at the beginning, but stick with it. I guarantee, you, dear reader, if you commit as much as three months to this, your level of attractiveness to almost *everyone* you meet will shoot through the roof!

Well, my friend, you've made it to the end! It's currently up to you to go off into the world with the confidence that your improved self-image is attractive to the people around you.

What's more, you now have the insight of the pitfalls to avoid if you wish not to turn people off.

Wherever you might be shaky (in terms of knowledge), I suggest going through the individual chapters again, to get a better grasp on the specifics.

Remember, the key is to *apply* what you learned. If it just stays in your head, you won't see *any* changes. Finally, I urge you, like with any powerful information you learn, to use it for good and not evil.

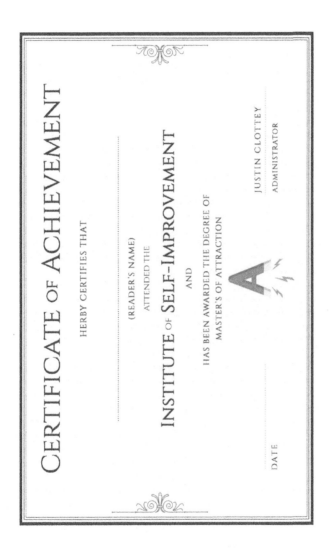

CERTIFICATE OF ACHIEVEMENT

HERBY CERTIFIES THAT

(READER'S NAME)

ATTENDED THE

INSTITUTE OF SELF-IMPROVEMENT

AND

HAS BEEN AWARDED THE DEGREE OF

MASTER'S OF ATTRACTION

JUSTIN CLOTTEY

ADMINISTRATOR

DATE

About the Author

Justin Clottey was born in the United States. He spent different periods of his life in various cities within Canada and around the world.

Justin considers himself to be a lifelong learner. Having an interest in constantly improving every area of his life, he is always looking for the best ways to do just that. The world of writing books to help people improve their own lives is an outlet he uses to live out his passion for teaching. As an elementary school teacher, he enjoys sharpening his talent for breaking down complex concepts into small, digestible pieces for his learners.

Justin has particular passions for fitness, sports, and language learning. These activities take up most of his free time. He speaks fluent English, Spanish, and French. He also enjoys spending time with friends and family as well as exploring different places.

JUSTIN CLOTTEY

Notes

_____

_____

_____

_____

_____

_____

_____

_____

_____

_____

_____

_____

_____

_____

_____

_____

_____

_____

_____

_____

_____

_____

_____

_____

_____

_____

_____

_____

IMPROVE YOUR SELF-IMAGE...

_____

_____

_____

_____

_____

_____

_____

_____

_____

_____

_____

_____

_____

_____

_____

_____

_____

_____

_____

_____

_____

_____

_____

_____

_____

_____

_____

_____

_____

_____

IMPROVE YOUR SELF-IMAGE...

_____

_____

_____

_____

_____

_____

_____

_____

_____

_____

_____

_____

_____

_____

_____